TRAVEL SAFETY

Safety tips for personal and corporate travellers

Craig Bidois
with Craig Martin

GW00691757

Travel Safety: Safety tips for personal and corporate travellers
By Craig Bidois with Craig Martin

© Craig Bidois and Craig Martin 2011

ISBN 978-0-473-20654-3

Published by Indie Travel Media Ltd
PO Box 5531
Auckland
New Zealand
http://indietravelmedia.com/

Production Manager: Craig Martin

Managing Editor: Linda Martin

Layout and Design: Angela Lees

Contents

About the authors

Craig Bidois

Craig Bidois is New Zealand's most experienced travel and personal security risk practitioner.

He is one of a select few certified to train United Nations executives in security, and one of the very few New Zealanders to be awarded the Iraq Reconstruction Medal by the British Government for his dedicated work under extreme conditions to help rebuild the Iraqi Security Forces. From humanitarian staff to corporate travellers, Craig Bidois has trained over 15,000 people in travel safety.

He currently serves as the Managing Director of **Fearfree (http://fearfree.co.nz)**, a New Zealand-based training and safety-monitoring company serving businesses around the world.

Craig Martin

Craig Martin travels. A lot. Since February 2006 he and his wife, Linda, have been virtually homeless as they travel around the world.

He brought his love of travel together with a degree in English Literature and Film, TV and Media Studies to create the award-winning website, **Indie Travel Podcast (http://indietravelpodcast.com)** which allows you to download travel "radio" shows and videos free of charge, as well as hosting a vibrant independent travel community. From there, Indie Travel Media Ltd took off as a niche travel-publishing company, serving hundreds of thousands of readers each year. He's been pick-pocketed, caught in earthquakes and sucked in by scams, and has learned from all of it.

Bringing together Craig Martin's independent travel experience with Craig Bidois's professional expertise in travel safety training, Travel Safety is a book that's realistic, practical and fun to read. Let's get into it.

The world is a safe place

(so why are we writing this book?)

Every year millions of trips take place: people leave their homes, travel and return without incident. In general, the world is a safe place and moving over borders and into foreign countries is safer than it has ever been in the history of the world. However, if millions of travellers encounter no problems, a small percentage encounter the worst of humanity, or the worst that nature can throw at us.

Who is responsible for your personal safety? This question was asked of a group of senior officers gathered in Sudan for a peace-keeping mission. Despite the retort of a certain Rwandan Major, the correct answer is not "my mom". The correct answer is that **you** are. You have to look after yourself.

It's our pleasure to share our stories, our experiences, and the best practices devised by the smartest minds in security. We've stripped out the jargon and kept things simple and practical while covering a wide range of possible situations.

Airline safety briefings often include the line, "in the unlikely event of an emergency…" This book is a manual for those unlikely emergencies, written by people who travel often. Every traveller has a different strategy as to how to look after themselves while they are on the road; we've brought together our experiences with stories and ideas from dozens of others. We only include advice we believe in, which has been road-tested by people who have survived traumatic experiences, and from those who have learned from all the little problems one might encounter while travelling.

Some people are more scared than excited by the world around them. It's not our goal to make you one of those people. It's our goal to help you become fear-free, by having access to the tactics and knowledge that will keep you safe. Don't be afraid to travel, to meet people, to immerse yourself in life and in the colourful cultures of the world. And if you ever come across the Rwandan military, it seems they actually have a sense of humour!

Up-to-date and online!

The topics discussed in this book are kept up-to-date and online.

Visit **http://indietravelpodcast.com/travelsafety** for more information.

SAFETY BASICS

What everyone needs to know

Taking care of yourself

A lot of travel safety comes down to good practice in what some would call "common sense". The only problem is, you develop this common sense from years of actually travelling, picking up little tips here and there, learning from mistakes in many situations. This first section of Travel Safety attempts to show you all these little "common sense" learnings we've picked up from years on the road.

There aren't many books in which the author hopes you only have to use one section, but this is not your ordinary book. We'd be very happy authors if you never encounter crime or dodgy dealings; we'd be ecstatic if you had no problems at all! These tips are designed to make your everyday travels as smooth and secure as possible, while later sections deal with the unpredictable experiences we hope you'll never have to face.

Your security research

Before you go on your trip, you'll probably use guidebooks, blogs and travel websites to get an idea of where you'll go, what you'll see and a hundred other details. But make sure you also do some basic research into the current political and security situations for your destinations.

Take a look at the travel safety website your government publishes; be aware that the American and Australian sites tend to be a bit more aggressive than the British and New Zealand sites. Also, political decisions can affect these advisories: if a government wants to put pressure on a country, there's nothing like hitting their tourism sector (and sometimes their financial risk rating) with a travel safety advisory… so take it all with a grain of salt.

Many governments allow you to register your travel plans online before you go. This allows them to know your approximate whereabouts in the case of a natural disaster or other emergency.

Consider registering your travel plans with this service, or call your foreign affairs office to find out what similar services your government offers.

For destinations that are particularly volatile or if you receive conflicting advice from official sources, buy a country- or city-specific report from a private travel security company. Fearfree provides inexpensive, impartial up-to-date bulletins like this: they can be worth their weight in gold.

Be streetwise

Some people just seem to attract trouble. A colleague of mine once burst into my office saying that his iPod had been stolen in a very poor area of an extremely poor country. When questioned further, it turned out that he had gone jogging after dark, outside the recommended safe area and outside curfew hours. He broke our security rules, and he also broke the rules of common sense: he put himself in the wrong place at the wrong time.

Strange things happen to people that push the rules just a little too far. Most of these recommendations are common sense, but sometimes our common sense goes on holiday at the same time we do.

- Avoid walking after dark by yourself, especially in isolated areas.

- Keep a low profile. Be conscious of using maps, cash and guidebooks in places where you are highly visible – you may get unwanted attention.

- If you think something is a threat, it probably is. Trust your instinct and take action. For example, if you think someone is following you, cross the street several times to confirm your suspicion. Go somewhere public, where there are people, and solicit help.

- Watch out for pickpockets, especially in markets and crowded areas. More advice for avoiding pickpockets can be found later in this book.

Blending in

It certainly pays to do some research about the country you are going to visit, including those you will transit through. Information is easy to find (try Google, or a library and bookstores), so there are few excuses for simple mistakes. With a little time, you can easily educate yourself about the local culture, customs and expectations. If you are time-poor, invest in a professional country report which includes cultural information.

Some important points to review before you arrive:

- **Dress standards in the country:** what is appropriate in your homeland may be disrespectful in another. Take a look at how people of this country dress, and discover what religious and cultural standards are normal.

- **Gestures:** Non-verbal forms of communication can smooth over a lot of language difficulties but can also put you at risk. What you may consider a friendly gesture may be a sign of great insult. I'm often reminded of language students I've taught flicking me the bird while saying the number two… that's not terrible in a language classroom, but could get ugly when ordering two beers at a seedy nightclub.

- **Greetings:** Learn how to say "hello", "goodbye", "thank you", and "sorry/excuse me" in the languages of the countries you'll visit. You don't need a language kit to do this: thirty minutes on a community site such as **italki.com** will be enough to get the basics and have a short chat with someone who speaks your target language.

- **Basic phrases:** You don't need a guidebook to learn how to say "thank you", but it might be worth investing in one if you want to go beyond the banal with the people you meet. You'll be surprised at how warm a reaction you get while trying to speak someone else's language.

The things we carry:
Documents and cash

For most travellers, the most valuable things you carry are your identity documents and whatever cash you have to hand. How to look after them is a topic which is often discussed, and sometimes fretted about. While they are certainly important, it's good to remember that you shouldn't allow yourself to be preoccupied by these items; and that your health is much more important than any object.

Documents

Losing your passport can be one of the most frustrating experiences that happen to a traveller. While I was travelling in Peru, my friend's daybag was stolen. Inside it were her most valuable possessions: camera, purse, ID cards, credit cards and passport amongst them. Our group was able to to support Jane with all the money she needed until new credit and debit cards could be sent out, but we weren't able to help much with the passport.

We soon realised that there's no New Zealand consulate in Cusco, and Jane was forced to get a temporary travel document issued through the British Consulate, while a new Kiwi passport was sent on to the Australian embassy in La Paz, Bolivia. If you've ever called a government agency, you'll know how difficult they are to deal with: now imagine trying to deal with three countries' offices, located in two other countries. That was difficult and stressful enough, but two weeks later we arrived at the border, temporary document in hand.

Jane's documentation only allowed her to travel on one day, and the only public transport to the border got us there early in the afternoon. The Peruvian border guards, however, were nonplussed by the documentation and wanted us to return to Cusco to verify it. You can see where that was heading… and it was no good at all. We did manage to talk our way over the Peru-Bolivia border with our non-standard but completely legitimate paperwork, but that experience reinforced the difficulty of losing your passport abroad. In short, we don't recommend it.

Essential documentation like your passport, visas and any medical prescriptions should be photographed or colour-scanned before you leave home. Email a copy to a few trusted and easily-reachable family members or friends, and make sure a copy of that email and attachment stays in your online email account. If you don't feel comfortable with storing these documents with your email provider, consider **dropbox.com** or another online storage system.

Many accommodation providers will ask for your passport when you check in. We suggest you carry a colour photocopy — witnessed by an official if you like — to give them. Most of the time, they just need to photocopy the details page or report your passport number to local authorities in any case. Sometimes they insist on your actual passport, and that's normally fine, but if there's no need for your passport to leave your possession, you might as well keep it close.

In inhospitable environments, copies of these documents can literally be a lifesaver. A woman was seriously injured in a motorcycle accident while I was working in Africa. Her wallet and passport were stolen at the scene, before she was found by security forces. She was in a grave condition, and no suitable local medical treatment was available. We needed to have her airlifted to another country for treatment, and urgently. Without any documentation at all, border control would not let her pass, no matter how we pleaded and threatened. They were doing their job — and a tough job it can be —, but a photocopy of her identification left behind by the thieves might have saved her life.

Carry your passport, or lock it up?

While you are in transit, it is best to carry your passport in a pocket that you can easily access, but which is difficult to pickpocket. A buttoned shirt pocket or interior jacket pocket is best, as you are unlikely to accidentally leave your shirt behind on the train! When moving from border control to your hotel, you might wish to use a security belt to hide your documents. Remember that the whole point of these is that they should stay hidden! Use a bathroom stall to hide your passport away, and don't take it out again in public for any reason.

Should you carry your passport at all times, or leave it locked in your room or with desk staff? Whatever you choose, you should never leave valuable documents (or other items) visible in your hotel room: it's too much of a temptation for staff if opportunity and availability are brought together like that.

At various times, we have chosen to leave our passports in locked bags in our rooms or in the room's safe, to leave them in hostel lockers, to leave them with desk staff and also to carry them around with us in a daybag or a hidden moneybelt. There's no right answer every time. The question is: which option gives you the most peace of mind? Or, which option gives the right amount of security over inconvenience?

I was once staying at a hostel in Istanbul, Turkey which didn't have lockers. Instead, we were told valuables could be left with the desk staff for safekeeping. I put my passport inside my laptop case and, after breakfast, dropped it off at the desk before heading out for a day's sightseeing in this amazing city. When I returned the desk staff had changed onto the evening shift, and no-one had any idea where my laptop and passport was.

I soon found out why: they weren't using a safe or locked cupboard to protect their guests' valuables, they were hiding these valuable items in a staff-member's bedroom. They looked under the bed, under the pillow and sheets, in desk drawers and in cupboards before they finally found my things. Needless to say, all my valuables came with me in a daybag the next day, and I looked after that bag very carefully. Some people say you shouldn't put all your eggs in one basket. Sometimes it pays to put them all in there and *watch that basket very carefully*.

If you have any questions at all about the reliability of desk staff, put all your things into a sealed envelope, then sign your name or draw a picture over the envelope's seal and get a receipt for that envelope before leaving. Recently, on the **Indie Travel Podcast Community forums**[1], one of our members reported that $300 left in an envelope with hotel staff mysteriously went missing from the hotel safe… you don't need Sherlock Holmes to solve the mystery, but you'd need him to get enough proof for an insurance claim.

At the end of the day, a room safe is normally very secure but if you are using any other option, you must balance your judgement on the safety of the area you will be in against the trust you have in the hotel staff.

Before you leave home:

- Colour-photocopy any important documents, including your passport details page.

- Colour-photograph or scan any important documents, email to a few trusted people, and store online.

- Write your first initial, last name and passport number on a few cards and keep them in your jacket pocket, bag, and wallet or purse. If copies in one place get stolen, you'll still have copies available to you.

---

[1] http://indietravelpodcast.com/forums

Insurance

With all the potential pitfalls of travel insurance, it's tempting to consider travelling without it. Our advice is simple: If you can't afford travel insurance, you can't afford to travel.

Your travel insurance needs will be completely different from everyone else's, and it's always a good idea to get several quotes and compare both the costs and the features of each policy. Some important questions to ask:

- Are the countries you are travelling to actually covered by your policy?

- If there's a natural disaster, civil unrest or an act of terrorism, does your policy still apply?

- What happens if you have to cancel your trip before you go? Because of illness? Business? Personal reasons?

- If your gear gets stolen, what will be replaced, what will be compensated for in cash, and are your expensive electronics covered? Most policies have a total value and per-item value limit, and differentiate between replacement value and retail value.

- If that stuff is lost or damaged rather than stolen, are you covered?

- Do you get evacuated in case of a medical emergency, or if the local services don't have the treatment you need?

- And while we're thinking about medical emergencies, what does happen when you get sick? Do you need to run your treatment past the insurance company first? Will they reimburse you, or do you need to work exclusively with their medical partners?

- Are you covered if you get sued or arrested while abroad? Does the policy cover legal expenses and any payouts?

- What activities aren't covered by your policy? Many don't cover adventurous activities… and "adventurous" might include a walk in the woods.

- Does your travel insurance cover you for accidents that happen while you are working?

- How much money can you claim if your documents are lost or stolen? Courier fees and replacement fees can get pricey quickly.

Insurance companies often have different levels of cover for medium- or high-risk countries. If you are heading into a country that might disqualify you from travel insurance, it's best to know in advance.

If you have already started your travel, and suddenly realise that you ought to get travel insurance, you might find difficulty getting it while you are overseas. In that case, we know **WorldNomads.com** allows you to buy, start and extend your travel insurance online. Their policies change for each country of origin, so we can't comment on the specifics of each policy, but it's a good place to start.

Once you have your travel insurance, you need to take a copy of your policy and store it online, just like with your passport and visas. Add your policy number and your emergency claim phone number to the card you carry in your wallet. There's no point having insurance if you can't access it in an emergency.

Cash

Cash is king, but it's also an obvious target for criminals. There are several strategies for minimising the risk of theft, and ensuring you have a backup when needed.

I often use a discreet money belt with cash and important documents inside. The trick with money belts are to make sure that they cannot be seen under your t-shirt or top. Use a skin-coloured belt so it will not be obvious, and wear a top that hides it completely. I have to laugh when I see people wearing skin-tight tops over a money belt at their waist; seeing someone layering back a tight top to muck around with zips, then displaying a thick wad of notes at their belly is unattractive to say the least!

With money and documents safely tucked away, make sure you have enough money for the day in your wallet or purse, or just loose in your pocket. This is the small amount of money that you can pull out for purchases, which ensures you're not flashing cash. If I'm just heading out for lunch, I keep the money I expect to spend in my shirt or trouser pocket… it's always safer to pull $15 from there than to bring out your wallet and show that you're loaded.

If you've underestimated how much money you need, or for some reason you need to access the documents in your money belt, head to the bathroom. Find yourself a private stall and move things around there: putting fresh cash or your documents in your pocket. There's no good reason to publicly show your money belt at any time. In fact, doing so completely negates the value of using one.

We were caught out by a lack of cash once. I was in a group of four travelling around Chile when a huge earthquake struck: the 2010 quake which hit 8.9 on the Richter scale at the epicenter, Concepción. We were 500 kilometres to the south, but we were affected by the loss of power and international telecommunications: while our Chilean friend was able to pull pesos from the ATM, we gringos couldn't get anything from our banks or, because the lines were down, use credit or debit cards to make purchases. We pooled our last remaining cash together and didn't let the guesthouse's owner know we didn't have his money. For two days we had enough for food and drink and, thankfully, we were able to withdraw money and pay our accommodation bill before moving in with some Couchsurfers who could look after us for a little longer. At that point we swore we'd always have enough money in our pockets for 48 hours of cheap food, drink and lodging.

Using ATMs to manage your cash just makes sense in most of the world. Travellers' cheques are horrible things that are often difficult to cash in, and they come with hefty fees. The same might be true of your bank, which will charge you per transaction: of course, you want to make the most of every withdrawal you make… but then you risk carrying around a large amount of cash for several days.

When you do use an ATM, do so quickly and in a business-like fashion. Don't stop to count money (unless you notice a large discrepancy), exclaim over your first bit of foreign currency, or anything else. Move the money from the machine into your pocket as soon as possible. After that, you might want to go to a private place and put a large amount of it in your money belt. If travelling with friends or family, split the money between you, to minimise loss if someone is stolen from.

- Do not use ATMs if there are suspicious people around, or if you are in a quiet or badly-lit area.

- Try to use ATMs during daylight hours, in a bank or busy public place.

- Have a plan to get your excess cash to a safe place soon.

- Needless to say, withdrawing a week's worth of money then going clubbing is a bad idea.

We met a traveller in Peru who had problems with money she withdrew in Bolivia. She had chosen to withdraw US dollars from the machine (an option in many South American countries) but there was something… not quite right about the notes. She believed they were forged (it was the smudge marks, she said, that really gave it away). And what can you do? You've suddenly got hundreds of dollars of scrap paper out of an ATM… go and find the nearest branch office? (Of a bank that stocks its machines with counterfeit notes?) Go find a cop? Call your bank? Nope, she headed straight down to the nearest exchange office and turned it all into Bolivian currency — she wasn't 100% sure of anything, but better safe than sorry was her thinking. We shudder to think what might have happened if she was caught passing on counterfeit notes.

Street crime and opportunists

If you are unlucky enough to have any problems with criminals during your travels, it's likely to be with opportunists: pickpockets and petty thieves who are after an easy, non-violent way to separate you from your valuables. In five years of full-time travel in fifty countries, pickpocketing has been the most common criminal problem we've encountered. And in five years, it has only happened to us twice.

Pickpockets

This advice will help you stay clear of most pickpockets.

- Always stick to well-lit and busy areas, but avoid public transport and stations during rush hour.

- Don't wander around with a map or guidebook in your hands: if you get lost, duck into a café to get your bearings.

- If you've only got today's cash in your wallet or pocket, you won't lose much. Some people carry a dummy wallet in their back pocket, while their real one is zipped inside a jacket pocket or carried in their front pocket.

- Don't carry, or show, valuable things in poor areas. Leave jewellery and electronics locked in a safe, not on display.

- If you use a moneybelt to store valuable documents and cash, keep it secret and keep it safe.

- Be especially alert in markets and, if anyone bumps you, check for your wallet… they might be that good.

- If you can handle the fashion faux-pas, consider buying trousers with zippable pockets: they make it that much tricker for pickpockets.

- Always lock bags with a sturdy padlock, and carry backpacks or messenger bags in front of you in high-risk areas.

Bag cutting

When pickpockets can't find their way into your bags through the normal methods of sliding open zips, they might take the risk of slicing open the bottom of your bag with a knife. This is often done by small groups, with many hands making quick work of all your possessions as they fall to the ground.

To deter this type of theft, use a bag with hefty material, rather than lightweight nylon or silk bags. Carry the bag in front of you, rather than on your back. Don't be seen to be putting valuable things into the bag and, if you are carrying laptops or electronics, put them into suspended pockets within the bag, rather than in the main compartment. Additionally, putting something bulky like a jacket in the bottom of the bag might stop things from falling out if it is cut open.

Some companies, such as PacSafe, produce bags with "slash-proof" features but you pay for this security with a significantly weightier bag.

Snatch and run

Snatch-and-run crimes are more aggressive, but normally non-violent. In these cases, the criminals will cut a strap, pull sharply to break a strap, or simply make a grab at a loose item such as a purse, smartphone or camera — then run. They might have partners to distract you or to slow down a chase, or they might use a motorcycle or scooter to race up behind someone and get away almost before you know what is happening.

At particular risk for these crimes are electronics hanging from neck straps, like DSLR cameras or MP3 players and cellphones on a lanyard. A quick-fingered person running a knife near the back of your neck is never a good thing, and the weight of these electronics mean they drop swiftly into their hand. Messenger bags looped from one shoulder are also at high risk, especially when carried behind you. You'll notice it going, but might not be able to do much about it.

Perhaps the most dangerous snatch-and-run technique is when criminals use a motorcycle or scooter. One person will drive, while the snatcher rides pillion behind them. They will drive up onto the pavement or target a person walking near the roadside and grab at a loose-hanging bag or handheld purse, relying on the speed of the bike to break any straps. However, occasionally the straps don't break, and the victim will be dragged along the roadside, unable to disentangle themselves.

It's very unlikely the criminals will let go of their prize: the tighter you hold, the more value they will assume they have found. Our advice in this case is to keep yourself as unharmed as possible: let go, get out of the straps, do whatever you must to avoid being dragged behind the vehicle.

Other tricks

There are all sorts of cons and scams practiced by professional criminals. They use tested scripts and a process of escalation, or sometimes just take advantage of a little naivety, to separate you from your money.

Once I was in the Middle East, walking in a city with a colleague, when a car stopped beside us. A lady got out of the car and asked me if I had change for a large note. Being a helpful person,

I reached for my wallet, but was cut off by my friend. He told the woman that we could not help, and steered me away. Her car was ready to go with a driver; I suspect she would have made a grab for my wallet and driven off.

A girl we met in Lima fell victim to a more sophisticated scam. She had been travelling without problems in South America for seven months and was coming to the end of her trip. As she was leaving another city, she was invited to visit a small shrine within the bus terminal. With nothing much to do, she accepted and went to visit, wearing a large pack on her back and a smaller one with her valuables — laptop, camera and passport included — across her chest. She entered the shrine with the two criminals she had been speaking with and looked around at the paintings and scarf-shrouded icon on an altar, and this is where it gets interesting. One of them — unknown to her — tucked a scarf from the icon into her backpack so as she turned to go the whole display tumbled off the altar and broke on the floor, to the horrified gasps of her guides. She put down her daypack and backpack in order to help pick up the pieces and, when she next looked, her daypack was gone, along with both the crooks. The shrine itself? Valueless: just part of the scam.

It's not unusual for anyone, even security experts, to be caught off-guard while travelling. Whether it's a vacation or a business trip, it's important to stay alert and be aware of your surroundings to avoid petty theft.

Run into a scam?

Help us by reporting it at
http://indietravelpodcast.com/travelsafety

If you are stolen from

What will you do if you are stolen from in this style of opportunist crime? Will you shout after the thief, and hope the people around you favour justice? Will you chase the offender down a street, down an alleyway, into their territory? Who knows where they might lead you, and what might happen then?

We recommend you act compliantly with street criminals. It's especially important to avoid confrontation with armed criminals — those with knives, guns or improvised weapons. After the robbery is over and the attacker is leaving, you can run away or shout for help as loudly as you like, but it's always better to walk away in safety than to fight back and risk serious injury.

In our first few hours in Santiago de Chile we witnessed rough street justice at work. A young teenager ran past, with shouts following him up the main street we were walking on. People flocked from shops to join other pedestrians on the street ahead and block the road. He was caught and given a severe beating while the handbag was returned to the young woman who had temporarily lost it. It was one of those experiences that showed us that life was very different here than back home!

A crime isn't normally followed by vigilante justice. The hours following a theft involve a trip to the police station, endless forms and questions — often through a translator — followed by a call to your insurance company, or an online claim form to fill in. If you are to have any luck with your insurance company, you must ensure that the police issue you with a statement of your claim.

It's always better to avoid being stolen from by being prepared and aware, than to confront a criminal at bay or end up spending hours working through police and insurance paperwork. Work these proactive patterns into your daily routine, buy gear with security in mind, and make these tips into habits that will help keep you — and your possessions — safe.

Crossing borders

Border crossings and transit stops are often difficult times for travellers. Weary from long journeys, and unfamiliar with local attitudes and conditions, it's the perfect chance for someone to take advantage of you. Always be especially wary at borders, as guards have almost complete control of the customs and border-control environment, while scammers love to look for targets in the entrance lobbies.

Airport transfers

If you have arranged a transfer from the airport or a venue, know the name of the people who will collect you. Some criminals will spot the name on your luggage tag and use it to gain your confidence; so use a luggage tag that needs to be opened to be read. Avoid being transported with anyone you have not been instructed to travel with.

Do not leave luggage unattended, and do not allow anyone else to help you with luggage while in a terminal or border area. Do not assist anyone with their luggage, either.

I remember arriving tired at the airport after a very long flight. A driver asked if I needed a cab and, before I could reply, he quickly took possession of my bag and walked out at speed. I chased my bag down to the very far end of the airport carpark, past the taxi rank, and into an unmarked vehicle. He drove like a bat out of hell, but we made it to my hotel without any unwanted diversions. Although I arrived in one piece, I'll never do that again: always keep control of your bags, and never get in an unmarked vehicle at any airport.

Plan your transits at times that are likely to be busy, or at least try to avoid the graveyard shifts. Late at night or very early in the morning, you're likely to have less options for transport, less people around to help you, and less support from police or guards than you might have during the day. Stopovers and border crossings during slow times or in small, isolated stations are never ideal.

Land borders

The area around land borders are generally not as tightly controlled as airports. Some land borders can be quite remote, leaving travellers at the mercy of the people who take them to the border, and those in charge of letting them leave and enter the country. Scams with fake visa offices, unofficial tariffs and drivers who take a very long way around are common, and especially well-noted in South East Asia.

Read up on the land borders you plan to cross using web searches or by asking on travel forums, like that hosted on the Indie Travel Podcast. If you are passing through a particularly difficult border, consider going with an organised tour group or banding together with a few other travellers before you go. Regular tours often have local 'fixers' on board who know how to grease the wheels and keep things smooth for their passengers.

If crossing a border by car, you might be asked to hand over papers, such as your passport and visas for checking. When doing this in a hostile environment, only open the window five centimetres: just enough to comfortably hand over your documents. You don't want anything thrown into your vehicle, or to give someone a chance to seize your keys or strike you.

We have known of cars being fired at because they have not recognized signals to stop at waypoints or borders. Those people in the roadside hut in the military gear aren't waving to say hi, they're probably local soldiers manning a waypoint. Always know enough of the local script to understand basic instructions like "stop", "checkpoint" and "passport check".

You might be doing this a lot

Remember that each transit point may require screening: you'll encounter it everywhere from airports to train stations and at almost every border you cross. Allow as much slack time in your schedule as you can afford: people make silly mistakes when they're running late for connections.

Travel as light as possible, with only a carry-on-sized bag if possible. Many long-term travellers prefer to travel without a large backpack or suitcase, as the minimal packing means they have less to lose in case of theft, and they save hours every time they change countries. This is especially true in airports and when crossing borders where smuggling or potential terrorism activities are being closely monitored. Pack light, with one bag, and you can save yourself a lot of problems.

Security proceedings can be time-consuming and bureaucratic, and often seem like a waste of time. We know, we've been there: In 2008, I travelled through over 20 countries, and if that's not enough time wasted in security, I don't know what is.

Don't get grumpy with security staff though: they're often paid poorly and are just doing their jobs. When people get annoyed at you, it doesn't improve the work you do for them, and it won't improve how border staff handle you or your possessions either. Treat them in a polite, professional manner, as they are following procedure to keep us all safe. If you don't like the procedure, the person you're talking with can't change it. And if you decide to make life difficult… believe me, they have many tactics up their sleeves to make you suffer!

Accommodation security

Your hotel room might be your home away from home, but it's also a strange place with potential risks. It might feel like your personal space, but dozens of other people may have access to it at any time. Cleaners, duty managers, maintenance staff and others might all have a key. It is wise to remember that you are not the only one who can access the room, and to take appropriate cautions.

You may be a little disorientated after a long flight and being in a new environment could increase your vulnerability. Listen to your gut feeling — if something doesn't feel right, take action or create time and space for yourself to figure it out.

Checking in

Some people need anonymity when checking into a hotel, but most of us mere mortals would never even think about that! No matter how famous you are or aren't, these tips will keep you safe and minimise the risk of identity theft or actual theft when checking in:

- Do not use your first name on documentation. Use initials to keep your full name confidential.

- Request a room that is located on the second, third or fourth floor: lower than second might allow unwanted visitors and above the fourth may be out of the reach of fire-fighting equipment.

- Request a room by the elevator to avoid long walks along the corridor.

- If you feel uncomfortable when visiting your room at any time, request that the Concierge assist you to your room. While the Concierge is with you, make sure the room is not occupied.

- Ask the hotel reception to inform you if anyone requests a room next to yours.

- Do not take the room if the reception staff announces your room number loudly. This may be a pre-arranged set up.

- When tipping porters or waiters do not display your wallet. Have small notes available.

> See the chapter on corporate travel safety if you might have to deal with virtual kidnapping or potential honey traps.

Room security

Whether you're in a five-star hotel or a five-dollar bungalow, you want your room to be a safe place. Use these strategies to ensure you harden the room against common security threats — from people and from unforeseen events.

- When you have settled into your room, explore your floor and hotel to get to know the surroundings. Take note of fire exits and count the number of doors between you and the exit.

- Always lock your door when leaving, even if for just a few minutes. If you are on the ground floor, avoid leaving the window open.

- A small rubber door stop placed under the door prevents others from entering your room while you sleep.

- Security peepholes in hotel doors are notoriously easy to reverse, allowing people to watch you in your room. A post-it note over the inside stops this from working.

- If someone knocks at your door, do not assume they are who they claim to be. Do not open the door until you have confirmed identity with reception. If you are expecting someone, make sure they are identified before letting them in.

- Keep your room key and number confidential.

- Avoid leaving the 'clean room' sign on your door: this alerts people to the fact you are not there.

- Leave your TV or radio on as background noise when not in your room to give the impression that you are inside.

- Secure your important documents and items at all times.

While on duty in Africa I was often worried by the security measures available when staying in private accommodation. I often decided to enter into private negotiations of my own, paying someone to sit outside my door as guard. While casual criminals might be deterred by this I knew that if any trouble was in the offing, my guard would disappear just as fast as he was able. And who's going to blame him?! I always gave my "doormen" a big shiny whistle: the kind a football referee carries around his neck. "Run," I'd tell them. "Just blow this thing as hard as you can while you're on the way." I never heard a whistle in the night, but the chance of a few seconds' warning was always worth the money... and the whistle.

Around the hotel

Hotels can contain many isolated areas which may lead to trouble for their patrons. Our last set of tips help you stay aware while wandering around the hotel.

- Before using elevators, ask yourself if they are reliable.

- If you are about to enter an elevator and someone inside makes you feel uneasy, do not enter or get off at the next floor.

- Don't leave valuables at the side of the pool while taking a dip. It's tempting to drop your iPhone on your towel while you swim, but it's likely to go walkabout. Take a paperback down to the pool instead, or make use of lockers when available.

- If you use the gym, be aware of your surroundings. Hotel gyms are often in isolated areas, which could leave you susceptible to an attack.

- If someone is following you, do not lead them to your room. Instead return to reception using the busiest route possible, and let your pursuer pass.

It's not only about theft

Having things stolen from your room might be a problem, but there are other potential threats. Kidnapping and sexual abuse are discussed later in this book, but let's take a moment to focus on the unsavoury tactic of a drug plant.

Laos is one of the safest countries in the world, with the exception of one town: Vang Vieng. It's one of the few places that I've sat down in a café and been offered a menu of illicit drugs rather than delicious drinks. While I was there, one traveller told me about a British couple who had just left: cleaned out by their accommodation providers and the police.

They left their apartment in the morning to spend a day inner-tubing down the river, and returned mid-afternoon to find that their still-locked room had been disturbed. Within a minute of them walking through the door, police arrived, entered and walked straight to an ashtray on a coffee table. An ashtray the Brits had never seen before. An ashtray containing a half-smoked joint. An ashtray which the police officer walked directly to.

With threats of jail, court time and fines — with the threat of missing their flight home in a few days — this young British couple were forced to negotiate a cash settlement with the police officers who so rudely interrupted their afternoon. They were driven to an ATM, made the largest possible withdrawal, and also handed over all the cash they had with them. If, as they suspected, the whole thing was cooked up between the police and accommodation owners, it was a profitable scam. After all, would a local judge believe the story of a young British couple staying in a town known for recreational drug use, or would they believe the evidence of police and accommodation owners? That's not a risk I'd like to take, and it's not a risk they were willing to take either.

The problem with these kinds of security threats is that they are almost impossible to stop, and almost impossible to protest. At the end of the day, you are the only one that can take responsibility for your security. Your embassy might be able to help, but the con artists are unlikely to let you out of their sight until they've got your money… and you sure won't get a police report with which to make an insurance claim!

TRANSPORT BASICS

Stay safe while on the road

Overland transport

Getting from place to place is, perhaps, one of the most enjoyable aspects of travelling. If you've ever caught the train through Austria, driven America's famous Route 66, or picked up a free city bike to cruise around Paris or London, then you'll know what I mean. However, transport can also be a danger area: as travellers we are unfamiliar with local systems, and often don't know which are the legitimate transport companies and which are known to be unscrupulous with their rates. We are unsure of what is normal, and what might be a danger sign. While that's always going to be the case, you can reduce the risk by following these tips.

Taxis

Taxis are essential for almost every trip: they take you to all the places you can't get to by public transport, they transport you directly and quickly to where you want to go. However, some taxi drivers are extremely unscrupulous, taking advantage of your visitor status and taking you for a ride — in both the literal and metaphorical sense. To cut down the risks associated with taking taxis in a strange city:

- Research your destination city beforehand using travel forums: what taxi companies are reputable, and what scams are currently being used?

- Where possible, use approved or registered taxis.

- Arrange transport before your journey by booking your pick-up or transfer online or through your hotel.

- Avoid unmarked taxis and those without radios.

- Sit in the rear behind the front passenger seat in order to have a good view of what the driver is up to. You can also exit quickly onto the footpath if, for whatever reason, a quick exit is needed.

- Don't forget to put seatbelt on – taxis can crash too.

- Pay the driver while you are still inside the taxi, unless you have luggage in the back.

- When paying, have exact change or small notes ready, and don't flash a pile of cash.

Theft by taxi

If, as happened to some friends of ours in Istanbul, the taxi driver drives around in circles for half an hour then pulls a knife to extort the full amount on the meter, you're best to just pay up. If their experience with "Rambo" is anything to go by, the police don't really have much hope of finding a rogue taxi driver in a city of millions.

One of the most-common problems with taxis isn't with unscrupulous drivers, it's with forgetful passengers leaving items in the backseat or the boot of the car. In some cases, those drivers have returned within an hour or two, searching for the foreigners who left thousands of dollars worth of gear in their cars. In other cases, you might as well try and find a needle in a haystack.

A colleague of mine in Austria was carrying a week's supply of expense money for the small team in his suitcase. Unfortunately, he left the baggage in the back of the taxi and only realised his loss after several minutes. There was no hope of recovering the money from the taxi company; luckily it was covered by insurance.

Feeling uncomfortable

If you feel uncomfortable while in a taxi, fake a phone call to a local friend or associate. Tell them how far away you are, and the name and number of your taxi driver, plus the vehicle's registration number. Repeat the numbers back to them as if they are writing them down. The "phone call" can give you piece of mind while keeping your taxi driver on the straight and narrow. If you feel really uncomfortable, it might be best to actually call someone!

If you don't have a mobile phone, don't worry — hold any piece of electronics up to the ear furthest from the driver and cover it with your hand as much as you can. If the driver realises you're talking to your camera … well, it's always good to have a laugh.

On the bus, train or minibus

Likewise, public transport is generally safe and secure but it can be an excellent platform for crime. The most common problem is pickpocketing, but muggings are not unknown during quiet times.

- Avoid travelling during rush hour — this is when thieves are most active.

- Keep an eagle eye on your items. A bike chain can help secure bags to luggage racks.

- Sit with other people, avoid empty carriages.

- Do some planning and know your way around to the best of your ability. Station maps are usually available online if you want to carefully prepare for the journey.

- Sit in the aisle, where you have an exit, not against the window.

- Move away if someone makes you feel uncomfortable. Do not become trapped.

It's always better to sit next to someone who looks respectable, than by yourself where a group of people can surround you. This is true of stations and airports as well: the number of times I feel I've found a quiet spot to relax in, only to have that quiet torn apart by the arrival of a big family or a muttering madman is too many to count! I've since given up on finding the quiet spots, and now stick with the crowd.

David, a friend of mine, was maybe a little too concerned about being mugged while travelling on the London tube network. It was the afternoon rush hour and he was standing, jammed into a carriage with dozens of other commuters. From the throng a hard, cold cylinder pressed into the small of his back: he was being held up in the middle of a tube carriage! Shocked by the gun barrel being held against him, he made a bit of a mess of himself; an unfortunately embarrassing reaction when he realised it wasn't a gun, but the end of an umbrella randomly prodded against him in the late-afternoon crush.

It's always good to be aware, but being paranoid about potential dangers can make anyone overreact to everyday events. At least people left David some more space after that, rush hour or not.

Coaches and long-distance buses

Long-distance coach journeys are often run by several tour operators with different prices and services. When choosing which company to travel with, you'll need to ask some questions. As well as the obvious ones about how long the journey is going to take and what food and drink will be served, there are some other questions to consider: the most important being the operator's safety record.

The internet is your best hope of finding out this information: do Google searches for the company name and ask specific questions about your route on travel forums. Remember that one person's bad experience shouldn't change your choice — every bus breaks down sometimes — but a range of bad experiences across an extended period of time indicates that this is not the company you want to be travelling with.

Driver exhaustion is one of the biggest causes of fatal crashes on long-distance routes. If your journey will last more than three or four hours, ensure that your bus has two drivers, or if there is only one driver, that the scheduled rest stops give the driver an adequate break.

Luggage security on coaches

When you travel by coach or long-distance bus, your bags are normally stored under the bus, while you sit above. While travelling in some South American countries, we found it was almost expected that thieves would riffle through the larger bags and backpacks people stored under the vehicle; we quickly learned to never store anything of value down there.

- If you've only got one carry-on sized bag, it's best to keep it with you.

- Cover your luggage with a lockable pack cover. Thieves will have to cut it open to access your bags.

- Always get a numbered receipt for your bag from the driver or conductor, to avoid arguments about ownership.

- Whenever the bus stops and the luggage door opens, keep an eye out for your bag walking off into the crowd.

It's not unknown for pickpockets to operate on long-distance buses, often stealing a bag or purse from a sleeping passenger and getting off at the next stop.

- Seats near the front of the bus provide more protection than those at the back.

- Seats near a stairwell or exit are particularly vulnerable.

- Wrap your bag's straps around your legs and hold it between your knees.

- If travelling in a group, have one person stay awake to watch your bags.

- Avoid getting drunk or taking sleeping pills if travelling alone.

Organised tours

Tour vehicles are generally very safe as the people using them are in a similar situation to yourself, and you are often travelling together for an extended period of time. If leaving valuable things behind in the vehicle, ensure that the vehicle is locked and that the driver doesn't leave keys with it. (Drivers from some companies commonly leave keys in the petrol flap or another "secret" place, so their guests can get into the vehicle if necessary.) Always keep your most valuable or irreplaceable things with you, in any case.

Rental vehicles

In most of the world, your biggest issues with rental vehicles will the same as driving at home: dangerous drivers and theft. Other risks are covered later in the book.

It can be difficult to adjust to dealing with road users who are less concerned about road rules, or the state of their vehicle, than you are. In many parts of the world, the road rules are considered more as guidelines… and the biggest vehicle often wins. Research driving conditions before you arrive, and watch behaviour carefully as you travel by taxi and public transport. Ask the rental agent about things that confuse you: give-way rules are often the most difficult to understand, and it's always good to check the open-road speed limit.

Don't forget the basics:

- Safety first: put seat belts on and be courteous to other drivers.

- Know what documentation you need, including vehicle paperwork, license translations, road taxes and insurance.

- Read up on local road rules or conventions before collecting your vehicle. Confirm anything you're unsure about with the rental office.

- Try to get a vehicle that will blend in with locally-owned vehicles.

- Fully check the vehicle before you leave on your journey. Report any unrecorded damage to the vehicle rental office.

- Keep the vehicle secured at all times. Never leave valuables in the car overnight.

- Keep attractive items out of sight, placing them in the trunk. Do this before you get to your destination to avoid unwanted attention.

- Most thefts are carried out by opportunists. If they see your items on the seat, they will smash the window and take them. Do not tempt them.

In rural areas you might encounter livestock like goats, donkeys or cows. Although they may seem wild, they are often owned, either by an individual or a community. In any case, it pays to remember you'll be driving through that community's territory for a long time: you don't want to commit a hit-and-run on livestock any more than you want to on a person.

You see some strange sights when you're working in a UN compound in Africa, but even I was surprised when two backpackers pulled up in a beat-up truck with a dead goat in the back. Driving along the track that served as a road, they had hit the goat as it grazed along the path. With no idea what to do, they chucked it in the back and high-tailed it to us. Within an hour, a crowd of locals had gathered outside the compound: the owner had discovered where his goat had gone, and he was there to collect compensation. He had brought a lynch mob with him, just in case it proved difficult.

We managed to negotiate fair compensation: the farmer was happy with the money he received, and the backpackers were glad to have settled things peacefully. The lesson here is to seek help when you can, and always try to compensate people for any damage you do. If those travellers hadn't sought our assistance they might have found themselves on the rough end of community justice, as well as having trouble on their subsequent journey through the tribal area.

Air travel

Before, during and after your plane trip

Air travel doesn't deserve the fear that many people treat it with — on the whole it is an extremely safe and effective way to travel long distances. Of course, you can rest a little easier by following some basic safety techniques to make things a little more secure.

Booking

When booking your flight, research the airline's safety record on Wikipedia or other websites. Most major international airlines have exemplary safety records, but smaller, local airlines might not meet the same standards. Although all operating fleets meet certain regulations and guidelines, don't assume that all airlines are equal when it comes to maintenance and internal security measures. Companies with a younger fleet tend to have fewer mechanical issues.

One seat on an aircraft isn't significantly safer than another, though if you are concerned about being able to exit quickly in case of emergency, choose a seat near the wing (for overwing exits) or near the front or rear of the plane.

Packing

Since 2011, carry-on luggage has been wrought with ever-more restrictions. Remember not to pack sharp objects, liquids in bottles larger than 100ml, or dangerous goods like fireworks or matches. Read your airline's guidelines about what you can pack in your checked luggage as well — this varies from country to country. Whatever you do, don't pack drugs or weapons.

Checked luggage

There are two concerns when checking luggage for a flight (apart from your bags being lost by the airline). One, that things will be stolen from your bag, and two, that someone will use your bag to transport illicit goods. The easiest way to avoid these problems is to travel with only a carry-on size bag. If at all possible, pare down your luggage to the 56cm x 45cm x 25cm standard carry-on size; not only will you remove the chance of the airline losing your luggage, you'll also have less to carry — which is good for your back.

Becoming an accidental drug mule — when someone uses your bag to transport illegal drugs — is a serious risk. One of the most famous stories of someone possibly having drugs planted in their bag is the case of Schapelle Corby, an Australian woman heading to Bali on holiday. She was stopped by Indonesian customs officials and 4.2kg of cannabis was found in her unlocked bodyboard cover. Jailed in 2005, she is not expected to be released until 2024 — despite her not guilty pleas; the lack of strong forensic evidence; and the testimony of John Ford, who overheard people describing planting the drugs in her bodyboard case. Even if you are carrying nothing of great value, it is important to lock your bags to prevent becoming a mule.

If you simply can't get down to carry-on size, you can use the luggage-wrapping service offered in many airports to encase your bag in clingfilm. This means that you will know if it has been tampered with as soon as you collect it. This service can be pricy and doesn't prevent customs agents from using a pair of scissors to get into your bag, but at least the chances of someone planting drugs in your bag is minimised.

Another option is to use padlocks on all of your bag openings. When choosing a bag, make sure to find one that has zips with two closures, preferably with an additional round section designed for passing padlocks through. Choose combination locks rather than ones with keys, and if you will be passing through the United States, make sure to buy TSA-approved locks. These are combination locks with a key hole at the bottom to allow TSA officials access to your bag if they suspect you to be carrying illicit goods. A padlock isn't completely secure, but it is a great deterrent. If someone is committed to break into your bag, a screwdriver or even a well-made pen can penetrate a zip, or a knife can slash open most luggage materials.

Make your luggage recognisable by tying a brightly-coloured ribbon to the handle or by choosing a bag with a distinguishing feature. This will make it easier to recognise when it's time to collect your bag, minimising the risk of picking up someone else's by mistake -- or of them taking yours. Make sure you have a luggage tag to help identify it in case of loss, but also ensure that your name isn't easily visible — con artists might use it to gain trust as they attempt to pick you up at your destination.

In flight

Securing your carry-on luggage

Flight attendants are generally a trustworthy group of people, but you still have to take responsibility for your possessions. It's not common, but flight attendants have been convicted of stealing from passengers' bags during flights.

In a well-publicised case, a first-class cabin attendant for Air France was arrested and charged with stealing from her guests in 26 cases stretching over a year; on one flight alone, passengers had over $5,500 stolen. The case is proof that "mile-high" thefts do occur, even if infrequently.

Because of this, it's necessary to be aware of your baggage in the air, just like you would on a public bus. Use padlocks on your carry-on luggage, and keep your bag locked if it is in the overhead locker or if you are leaving your seat.

Safety briefing

As the flight attendants say, you should listen to the safety briefing on every flight you take, regardless of how often you fly. Each aircraft is different and you need to know the emergency procedure for the one that you're on.

To help your exit in the case of an emergency, count the seatbacks from your seat to the exit, and take note of where the lifejackets are stored. The chances of you needing this information is extremely slim, but if you do need it you won't want to have to think about it for more than a second.

Be able to react

It's important to stay alert while travelling, so avoid drinking too much before or during flights -- a glass of wine with dinner shouldn't hurt though! Similarly, avoid taking sleeping pills if at all possible, and do not take them at all if you are travelling alone.

If you do decide to sleep, lock your bags and keep your valuables out of sight, preferably on your person. You'll want to arrive at your destination refreshed and ready to go, so set your watch to the local time at your destination as soon as you embark, and plan your sleep accordingly.

If you have chosen to sit in an exit row, stay sober and avoid sleeping pills. You may be called on to open the emergency exit and to quickly exit the plane. Being able to do this quickly and efficiently is your responsibility; not being able to do so puts other passengers at risk.

Disembarking

Many people stand and prepare to disembark as soon as the plane touches down, while it is still taxiing to the gate. Standing up to get your bags out of the overhead lockers isn't going to get you off the plane any sooner, and there's a risk of injury since the plane is still moving. Wait until the plane has come to a complete stop and the captain has switched off the "fasten seatbelt" sign before standing up.

Check for your passport and other valuables before you leave the aircraft, and try not to hit anyone else in the head while getting your carry-on bag down from the overhead locker. If you have heavy baggage, it is best to wait until the aisles have cleared to give yourself maximum maneuverability while recovering it.

Collecting baggage

If you have checked luggage, head to the baggage carousel to collect it, looking out for your bag's distinguishing features. If you believe that your bag has been tampered with, notify authorities straight away — preferably before opening it or handling it in any way.

A tourist visiting Japan was surprised to find cannabis in his bag after he arrived in his hotel room from Narita airport. He called the airport police and returned it… only to discover that a customs official had planted it in his bag as part of a drug-dog exercise! Not only did the officer break the law by planting the drugs, he also risked the passenger's life and liberty. Imagine if he was catching an onwards flight to Indonesia; he might have faced the same sentence as Schapelle Corby.

On the water

Be alert on the water

Cruising the lakes, rivers, canals and seas of the world is something special, but with special experiences come special risks. Weather and maintenance problems will have a much stronger impact on a water journey than if you are travelling by land. This was recently proven by our friend Kate, as she travelled in Indonesia.

Kate McCulley, who blogs at **Adventurous Kate**[2], was on a multi-day boat trip when her vessel was driven into the rocks. The captain was attempting to navigate a dangerous channel at night during bad weather. The passengers included a young family with a baby, several backpackers, and Kate herself — who was on a press trip. All too late the passengers realised that the lifejackets were hard to get to, and that there were no other flotation devices.

As the boat listed in the water the crew instructed passengers to make their way to the front of the boat where they jumped into the water and swam through choppy water to a rocky shore. The baby's father tied the child to his wrist and a life jacket before attempting the swim. Thankfully, all the passengers made it ashore, but now they faced a different problem. The island they had swum to was Komodo Island — known for its fearsome, poisonous dragons. It was dark, they were wet and cold, and they were trapped in a hostile environment with some of the scariest reptiles on the planet.

Although they were poorly prepared for the disaster, we can be thankful that Kate, her fellow passengers and all of the crew survived the night and were rescued the next morning by another boat.

[2] http://adventurouskate.com

Unfortunately, there was more to come for our unlucky passengers. When their luggage was recovered from the stricken ship they found they had been robbed by the crew. Their bags had been ransacked and stuffed with biscuit packets and other rubbish. Although everyone survived, this was still a tragic end to what should have been a fun cruise through the islands.

Surviving shipwreck

Once you are out on the open water, you really have to look out for yourself. In many parts of the world, safety standards are not what you might expect, and an operator promoting themselves as "the safest" only has to have lost one fewer vessel than their competitors. While you needn't be suspicious of every ferry provider, it is best to:

- Research the safety record of the company you plan to use. Sometimes a more-expensive choice is worthwhile.

- Know the weather report and, where possible, the marine report for the areas and times you are sailing.

- If locals are concerned by the weather or a particular route, trust their judgement: rebook for another day.

- Captains will sometimes take huge risks for your money. Don't put their lives in danger for a pleasure cruise or to stay on your travel schedule.

- If lifejackets are scarce, or the boat unsafe, don't get on board. Find another operator.

- If all options are bad, and you choose to go ahead, take a lifejacket as a cushion early on.

- When dressing for a water journey, imagine yourself swimming in those clothes. Then get changed into something more suitable.

- Shoes and bulky clothes will drag you down if you need to abandon ship. Remove them before getting into the water.

- Keeping valuables (like your passport) in a waterproof, roll-top bag will mean it's easy to grab and run if you need to abandon ship. Air trapped inside can offer a little extra floatation, but this is not to be relied upon.

GETTING SPECIFIC

Safety advice for your travel style

Safety tips for corporate travellers

While corporate and government travellers face the same everyday dangers as other travellers, there are specific issues that warrant attention. The risk of kidnapping is higher for corporate travellers, as is the risk of entrapment or the emerging threat of virtual kidnapping.

While kidnapping itself is covered in a later chapter, *When Violence Strikes*, here we will focus on entrapment and virtual kidnapping. Both types of attack aim to extort money, or to influence the decisions of your business or government.

Corporate and business travellers are not only responsible for their own safety, but for the reputation of the entity they represent, and the data they are entrusted with. Money is always on the line but the greater threat is often to the information you carry or the decisions you or your business are going to be making.

The two most common scenarios, outlined below, are the honey trap and virtual kidnapping. These are used with great success by organised criminals around the world, but can be avoided if you recognise the risk and disentangle yourself from the situation.

The honey trap

Business executives, male or female, may be the target of calculated entrapment to obtain information or favours. The 'honey trap' — where a person is lured into a compromising personal situation in their hotel room or another location, then robbed, extorted or both — is the most common form of entrapment.

The criminals who practise this form of extortion are professionals, often working as part of an organised crime syndicate. They are practiced and well-resourced, which makes them very efficient. They also have specific goals, such as to steal a laptop or to obtain compromising evidence to be used in the future.

The honey trap is efficient not only in business, but also in government and military espionage. Even the appearance of evil can damage a career in a field that carefully guards its secrets, as was discovered by a still-unnamed Swedish officer accused of passing NATO secrets on to her Serbian lover in 2007. It can even lead to death — as in the case of the infamous Mata Hari, who was executed on the basis of flimsy evidence: the fact that a German officer was sending her money. She claimed until the end that he was her lover.

It's always flattering to be approached in a hotel bar or when out and about, but you should always be wary of taking people back to your room; this is never a recommended practice when it comes to security. The person — the bait — may be glamorous, and will certainly be well-versed in flirting and drinking. There are no definite tell-tale signs that can help you distinguish a fun flirt from a dangerous situation: to avoid the risk of the 'honey trap' always be polite but not too friendly with people who you do not know and who are interested in spending intimate time with you.

Virtual kidnapping

Virtual kidnapping is a recent development in extortion which is especially popular in Eastern Asia, Mexico and Brazil at the moment, although the practice is beginning to spread around the world. During a virtual kidnapping, the victim doesn't even know they're in trouble, but their families or work colleagues certainly think they are… and that's where the criminals make their money.

In a traditional kidnapping, the victim is identified, captured, and transported to a holding space, after which negotiations are entered into and — hopefully — the victim is rescued or released. The logistics of transporting and holding even one person need to be carefully thought through, and the gang must have enough cash to last through the negotiation period and beyond. You need access to property, food and drink, guards and accomplices… It's a big outlay and a lot of work.

On the other hand, a virtual kidnapping — also known as a remote-control kidnapping — relies on having information about the target, and limiting the target's access to their normal communication channels. Virtual kidnapping greatly reduces the risks criminals encounter, which means it can be done by smaller gangs working with small budgets. This is obviously bad news for the business traveller, because it increases the chance of becoming a victim. The story below shows how easily this game can be played on an unwitting set of victims: the mark and his or her colleagues.

Meetings have finished for the day, and an executive — bored of the hotel room — heads out to a local bar. He talks with a few people and, eventually, this victim gives their business card to someone they meet. This contact passes the card — and any other personal details they've discovered — to a courier who passes it on again, and a negotiator calls the victim's office (or home). The victim's colleague is told that their workmate has been kidnapped and is being held hostage, and that the company has a very short timeframe to pay the ransom.

The criminal who calls to make the ransom demand will use any trick possible to ensure payment. They have reliable facts: where the person is, what business they're working for, personal details gleaned from the conversation. In some cases, a recording of someone screaming and crying is played in the background for emotional effect. The criminal's goal is to have the call passed on to someone who can make a payout decision, then to pressure that person into authorising a money transfer as quickly as possible.

The victim is blissfully unaware — probably on their second or third beer by now —, and the role of his new-found friends is to keep him in the bar (or away from the hotel), and stop him from answering his cellphone. In some cases, the cellphone is stolen earlier in the day or while at the bar, and can even be used to make the ransom demand. Often, details from the ongoing conversation are passed on to the criminal negotiator to strengthen their claims.

This false abduction relies on information being available to the criminals, the 'victim' being out of contact, and on the shock tactics applied by the negotiator. If you can stop your private details getting into criminal hands, stay in touch with key contacts (at work and at home), and if businesses have a policy in place for handling ransom demands, you greatly minimise the risk of being taken in by this scheme.

Virtual kidnappings also occur outside of the travel sphere. There are rising reports worldwide where jailed criminals threaten the wellbeing of other inmates, unless the victims' families make payments to secure their safety. Parents are targeted when their teenage children fill in entry forms to win a new gadget outside shopping centers. A physical description of what the child is wearing along with the personal information on the entry form is used in negotiation; those calls are made while the teenage victims are in a movie theatre: it's good form to switch your phone off for those two hours, which means the criminals have a perfect window of opportunity.

Ransom calls might be made to family members, colleagues, or both: whoever the criminals think have access to money. If you are heading to a high-risk area, it may be worth discussing the possibility of virtual kidnapping and a good response with people at home. Your business should also have a policy in place to protect your safety. Do you know what it is?

A virtual kidnapping can sometimes be foiled as easily as making a call to the supposed victim's cellphone — but it's best to have professionals on your side. If you ever receive a ransom call, make sure to contact your security specialist or the police immediately.

Why haven't I heard about this?

At Fearfree, we provide tracking and emergency response teams for many corporate and government clients. Of all the calls we get, at least 50% come from people who are travelling in non-threat locations. That is, places that are politically stable and have first-world amenities, infrastructure, policing and justice systems. Remember that just because you are in a developed country does not mean you can let your guard down. General crime like theft, assault and disorderly conduct occur in every part of the world, and so do the specific types of corporate crime we've discussed in this chapter.

You might not hear much about it… no government or corporation is likely to admit that they have had secrets stolen or money extorted from them. There's a media blackout of a kind, as large entities try to deal with the fallout in-house and avoid public scrutiny and speculation. That doesn't mean the threat isn't real. You should certainly be aware of the scenarios discussed above and, if you have further questions, talk with your company's security advisory team before beginning your trip.

Duty of care

Your company has a legal Duty of Care towards you, to cover them under health and safety laws. This is often bolstered by further clauses in their insurance policies. They should brief you on local laws, customs and normal behaviour to help you minimise the inherent risks of travel. You should make sure you understand your company's travel policies, and be comfortable with the level of support they give you when you are on the road. At the end of the day, though, you are the one making the decisions, and you must be responsible for the outcomes, no matter how strange or unexpected the situation is.

If your company needs help in devising security strategies and policies for your staff, contact co-author Craig Bidois at **http://fearfree.co.nz.**

Safety advice for vacationers

It's always great to head out on a vacation, whether a weekend break or a week or two away. There's always the chance to do something new, spend some time relaxing, and enjoy the food, the smells and the specialities of the places you are visiting. As well as following the general advice in previous chapters, be aware that vacationing has its own special risks.

Watch what you drink

The start or end of your holiday is a perfect time to cut loose, but watch how much you are drinking!

Orson Welles once said there are only two emotions on a plane: boredom and terror. If there's a need to feel terrified, you don't want to be drunk and slow at the same time. Take it easy when flying, especially since the higher altitude can amplify the effects of alcohol.

Criminals keep an eye out for easy prey, and the combination of being a stranger to local customs and being drunk definitely makes you a prime target! Whenever you are drinking heavily, make sure you are in trustworthy company and that you have a way out — even if it's just the phone number of a taxi company in your pocket.

But its not just crime — alcohol plays a part in many other incidents. Raucous Brits abroad have become such a problem in some cities, like Krakow and Riga, that kilts have been banned. Certain Scots would drink themselves to the point where flashing passersby seemed like a good idea. A few years ago in Riga one drunk young man earned himself five days in jail after urinating on a monument… not the best way to spend your holiday.

Save yourself a visit to the cells or a call to your insurance company, and know when to stop.

Are you really insured?

Talking of insurance, are you really insured? And what for? Take the time to revise the section on travel insurance to make sure your policies cover you for the type of activities you'll be doing, in the countries that you'll be doing them.

Why are they looking at you like that?

In many countries, you will stand out. From your skin colour, to your physique, to the clothes you wear, it's hard to not be seen as a foreigner. That's not too much of a problem, but you might bring problems upon yourself if you refuse to acknowledge and respect local customs.

I once passed through Istanbul in Turkey on the way to a work appointment. I had a few days to stopover in the city with my wife, Linda. Our briefing included instructions on women's dress: it should cover the shoulders and be reasonably modest. I was quite surprised to find that Istanbul isn't a hotbed of conservative dress, however much some factions would like it to be. A girl in a miniskirt walked beside another in a full-length dress and a headscarf; a guy in shorts and sandals chatted with another in pressed trousers and well-shone shoes.

As tourists visiting Istanbul we certainly felt more comfortable taking a conservative tack: the most vociferous public opinion definitely came from the religious conservatives, and we didn't want to do anything to draw extra attention to ourselves. Follow the customs of your hosts — try not to stand out too much, or to cause offense. At the end of the day, you are a visitor in someone else's home.

Round-the-world and long-term travellers

Those who travel for an extended period of time — for one month or longer — often have a different sort of agenda. Instead of sightseeing from hot-spot to hot-spot, the independent traveller is likely to drift more, have less of an itinerary, and be more likely to stay with locals or stray from the beaten path. They tend to be more relaxed about their destinations, but long-term travellers also face important travel safety issues.

Facebook fraud

I recently read about a backpacker who was travelling through South East Asia. She had spent some time in an internet café before heading to her hostel and hitting the sack. She needed an early night: the next day she started a week-long hiking trip in Thailand.

At some point — probably soon after she left the internet café — criminals struck. Hacking into her Facebook account, they were able to plot her family relationships and contact her parents. The private Facebook message claimed that she was hospitalised and needed money wired to her immediately to pay for the stay. Since she was unable to leave the hospital, the money could be sent by Western Union to a name the criminals supplied.

Her parents, obviously concerned, messaged back to console their damaged daughter and, with a few facts checked and everything seeming legitimate, started organising the money for a Western Union transfer. It was quite a surprise when their daughter called on the day they were to transfer the cash: hale and hearty having returned from her hike.

Cyber theft

There are simple precautions to take whenever using a strange computer — signing out of accounts, using a private browser window, using https, clearing cookies, carrying your own browser on a USB stick, or using a password manager with a secure copy/paste function. However, there is a risk of passwords being stolen whenever you are using other people's computers or surfing on an unsecured wifi network. Facebook, for example, recently reported that up to 600,000 logins were compromised each day. They didn't elaborate on exactly what they meant by 'compromised', but we can assume a fair portion of that figure refers to stolen passwords.

I don't know whether this family's situation was caused by keylogging software (which records every key you hit on the keyboard) or by her forgetting to sign out of Facebook. I do know that a little more communication might have saved the day; if you are normally online, let close friends and family know when you'll be offline for an extended period of time. And if you ever receive an email like that, talk to the person on the phone before sending money.

RTW trip planning

It is a sad state of affairs, but some countries really don't trust their neighbours — and this is something to take into consideration when planning your round-the-world itinerary.

The best-known example of this is the borders between Israel and the Arab League — once you have a border stamp from an Arab League nation, it will raise questions when you cross the Israeli border. Even worse, the following countries may refuse entry to anyone with an Israeli passport or with an Israeli stamp in their passport: Algeria, Bangladesh, Brunei, Djibouti, Iran, Kuwait, Lebanon, Libya, Pakistan, Saudi Arabia, Sudan, Somalia, Syria,

United Arab Emirates, Yemen and Malaysia (you might be able to get clearance for Malaysia in advance)[3]. Now that's a lot of places to consider when planning your RTW flights!

You can ask the Israeli border control not to stamp your passport, but there's no guarantee that they will agree not to, so it's best not to have plans that force you to fly out of one of these countries unless you can change your tickets. Your pre-trip research should dig up any other current inter-country issues that might cause problems at the border control.

Going home with someone

One of the most lovely things about travelling without rush or plans are those serendipitous moments when you fall into conversation and hit it off. It's not unusual to be invited back to someone's house for a family meal — not because they want something from you, but because you're interesting and they take pleasure in hosting visitors to their country. There are always times when this can go wrong though: take the case of the card-game con, which is popular in Ho Chi Minh City at the time of writing.

You are approached in the street and asked where you're from — the person knows something about your home town or a nearby city because, coincidently, their sister is heading there to study nursing. They ask if you'd be willing to meet her, and talk to her about life at home. Eventually, you end up back at their house for lunch, only to find out that she's at work. This is a pretty common opening, practiced around the world.

In this case, it escalates when an uncle comes into the room. There's time to kill, so he offers to teach you a card game — which you are surprisingly good at. You are invited to a game later that day and — after a visit to an ATM — you are separated from your money. The separation is normally in the form of

[3] http://en.wikipedia.org/wiki/Arab_League_boycott_of_Israel#Passport_restrictions

losing every bet to the cheating card sharks, but the option for violence is still there.

The moral of the story is to trust your gut feeling, to not be too trusting, and to never play cards for cash with strangers.

......

If you are travelling solo or for a long time, you might start to feel isolated and without support. If you do have a bad experience, don't let that ruin the rest of your trip. Take the time you need to process it, talk with friends, try and get something positive from it, and keep going. Sometimes things don't go to plan, but that's part of the journey.

You can read about scams and cons which are currently in vogue, or report others you hear about, at **http://indietravelpodcast.com/travelsafety**

Solo travellers

The main safety issues that affect solo travellers revolve around one fact… you are alone. There's no-one you can trust to challenge your judgement calls, no-one to report that you didn't come back to the hotel, no-one to pour you a glass of wine when you're feeling down. On the other hand, solo travel can be one of the most enjoyable, liberating experiences you'll ever have, so we certainly don't want to discourage you from going!

To battle isolation, develop a virtual network of friends and family members that you check in with regularly. You can use email, Skype or your favourite social networks to stay in touch and let them know what you're up to. This will also help friends to keep tabs on you in case there is a problem, and to stop security issues like the Facebook hacking we described in the RTW travel chapter.

You can also make use of the natural social networks you'll find as you travel: expats, fellow travellers, hostel owners and hotel concierges can all do their bit to keep you company and keep you safe. As always, trust your instincts and have fun. As we've travelled around the world, we've often met up with travellers and decided to spend a few days together: bussing around the Baltics or enjoying lazy days by the beach, our travels have been enhanced by those we spontaneously connected with.

Do not be too trusting of strangers who approach you to become your new best friend. Take a look at some of the travel scams in the round-the-world chapter, and also the up-to-date stories at **http://indietravelpodcast.com/travelsafety.**

Your plans and your friends

How will friends and family know if you are in trouble? Have you spoken to them about how you might contact them, or who they should speak to if they suspect something is wrong? It's certainly a good idea to let them know if you are going to drop out of contact for a while, and also to let them know your plans and when they might expect to hear from you again.

If you are travelling for an extended period of time, it's going to be impossible to leave an itinerary with someone you trust; but if you have a set plan, consider doing so. The itinerary should include details of the hotels you intend to stay at and the flights or other transport you'll be using. This will help your friends keep you safe, and can save potential panic if a crash or fire near you is reported in the media.

An emergency out

It's always good to have an emergency budget — at least enough money to buy a flight home immediately —, but this is especially important for solo travellers. Since you don't have a partner or group of friends looking out for you, you need your own resources that you can use to pay for emergency services or an unexpected change of plans. A natural disaster such as flooding or an earthquake can leave you out of pocket when you have to cover the costs of cancelled or missed flights, extra accommodation costs, and an itinerary that's impossible to recover.

Hopefully your insurance company will have your back, but they don't all cover expenses brought about by an 'act of God'. Even if they do cover these costs, you might need to pay for everything up front then claim it back later, so having access to an emergency fund is still essential.

Likewise, it's good to have your exit plan in place in case you arrive somewhere that is particularly unpleasant. Do you know where you'll go next? Is there another hotel or hostel you can move to in a hurry? How can you move on to the next city?

There are tens of thousands of people travelling solo at any given time. Whether you are a business person heading into London for a meeting or a backpacker overlanding in Africa, travel safely and stay in touch with the people you trust to look after you.

Solo women travellers should take a look at the Art of Solo Travel, published by Indie Travel Media at http://artofsolotravel.com.

WHEN VIOLENCE STRIKES

Surviving deadly threats

Being taken by force

Kidnapping, motivated by political or criminal goals, appears to be on the rise, although most ordinary travellers will never encounter it. Professionals and politicians are a richer source of money, media coverage and political leverage than backpackers and family travellers, so they are more likely to become victims; tending to be targeted around transit and conference areas.

A female humanitarian, Cara, once told me of how she was captured in the Middle East. She was not one to break the rules and normally followed the safety guidelines to the letter. As these things go, the first time she did bend those rules, she ran into serious trouble.

Soon after her driver departed from a prescribed safe route, they were stopped at gunpoint and forced into the trunk of another car. As the two prisoners were driven on, they could hear the sounds of traffic and trains. Eventually the car stopped and they were blindfolded before being bundled into a house, where they were separated and put into different rooms. Cara knew they were being held near a seaport as she could hear the toots of the ships as they exited the port. She was held captive for some days before a negotiation took place and they were released.

Her guards were quite lax late at night, and at one point Cara had the opportunity to escape. But she decided not to. Why? Because she had no idea where she was; no idea if the people around the holding house were friendly or not. Maybe she would be in a more extreme environment if she was found by others in the area. Cara was also worried about what would become of her driver if she escaped. There were too many risks, and staying put was the wisest decision in this case.

Understanding kidnapping

Your job in any hostage situation is simply to survive. It is probable that other people are working to have you released, but in the meantime, you must stay alive. There are commonly five stages to a standard kidnapping and hostage situation: capture, transport, holding, release and aftermath. By understanding these stages, you give yourself the best chance of a good outcome.

1. Capture

Capture is the first and most dangerous stage as it is often quick and violent, led by people with itchy trigger fingers ready to do serious harm should you not comply with their demands. The attackers will be stressed and full of adrenaline, making them unpredictable and violent. Your options are to resist and retreat, or to comply.

If you resist and retreat, you need to be confident that you can overcome your assailants and escape. You must be prepared to fight like hell, then get away. You have to weigh up the potential risks to yourself and to those with you, who might be left behind with the kidnappers.

If you decide to comply with your attackers, it is important to remain calm. We also advise avoiding eye-contact. It sounds silly, but your calmness communicates itself to the attacker: they feel in control and are therefore less likely to injure you. Abusing your attackers or making demands will aggravate the situation. There will be a time and place for controlled discussion and negotiation, but not just yet.

2. Transport

Sometimes rough handling is endured during this stage — maybe you'll be put into the rear of a vehicle, possibly blindfolded and handcuffed. Remain calm while you are being moved, and try to identify the area you are in by listening carefully. Can you hear vehicles or animals? Are you near an airport, a busy road, a port, or in a rural area? Any information you can safely gather may be useful later.

3. Holding — being a good guest.

Many former hostages emphasise the need to remain positive, as hard as it may be. Try to develop a routine for yourself and exercise both mentally and physically. Humanise yourself, let your captors know that you are a human being — you need to wash, eat, write, exercise. As time goes on and you become familiar with the people and your surroundings, consider starting to talk about your fears, your favourite sport, or your family. It is easy to kill an 'animal' but if you are seen as human being then you increase your chance of survival. Avoid political and religious discussions.

One of my colleagues from Croatia always said he followed football not because he liked the game, but just in case he was taken. He'd then have something to talk about with his captors, hopefully improving his treatment and lessening the risk of the situation. This wouldn't have worked for me, I follow rugby!

My friend Cara survived her hostage situation by staying calm and compliant, showing her captors that she was human and hoping for release or rescue. On another case I worked on, a group of contractors were taken and held for a number of months before being rescued by security forces. Sadly, one of the group did not survive captivity. Why was one killed? He was a constant irritation to his captors: always complaining, threatening and being unhelpful. The captors eventually lost patience with him, and he lost his life.

To sign or not to sign

Your captors may want to obtain a confession or press release from you. It is your decision whether to proceed — but remember, your objective is to survive. You will probably disagree with what you are asked to put your name to, but your family and friends will not hold it against you, knowing that you were coerced.

Break free?

If the option is open, you may consider escape. Points to consider before such action:

- Where exactly are you? Do you know the area? Is the local environment better than where you are being held, or is it just as hostile?

- What about anyone else left behind — what will their fate be if you escape?

Stockholm syndrome

When you spend a lot of time with someone, you are more likely to develop an affinity for them. Although it seems unthinkable, in some hostage situations, especially lengthy ones, the captives begin to agree with the ideals and demands of their captors. This phenomenon is known as Stockholm syndrome, named after a situation some years ago in Sweden where the hostages became in agreement with the hostage takers. Don't feel bad if this happens to you, but remember to focus on your goal — survival.

Language

I am often asked: if you know the local language being used by the captors, should you keep quiet and use it to your advantage or should you try to talk to them to break the ice? My answer is always: you will have a feel for the situation — use your instincts.

I know of one case, however, in which a hostage who spoke the local language decided to keep quiet and the captors became suspicious. The hostages were lined up and the captors said (in their language) that they were going to kill the prisoner with brown shoes. The hostage glanced down at his feet without thinking, revealing that he could speak the language used by the hostage takers; the story doesn't end well.

4. Release from captivity

The good news is that most people are released, normally by negotiation or rescue.

Should a rescue be attempted by government special forces, it is important to take cover and keep quiet. The rescue team will take control of the situation and you should wait for the action to die down before revealing yourself. Safety first: do not jump up announcing the fact that you are a hostage, as sudden movement may attract automatic gunfire in your direction.

5. After the events

Depending on the situation, and on the policy of your government or corporation, you might find yourself approached by the media to discuss your experience. If you are expected to talk, do it in your own time. You need to rest and regroup.

As soon as possible after the events, visit a professional counsellor, even if you don't feel like you need to. You may be suffering from post-traumatic stress disorder and a professional counsellor can help you with this.

Avoidance is the best medicine

Of course, the best way to deal with a kidnapping situation is to avoid it altogether. Use your common sense: avoid danger zones, keep a low profile, and don't be predictable.

However, if you are kidnapped, remember that your primary goal in a hostage situation is to stay alive. Do what you must to survive.

Armed robbery

You are probably more likely to encounter an armed robber at home than when abroad, but for many people this type of crime is associated with travel. Whenever I speak with family before or during a trip, they always say: "Be careful, don't get mugged." This seems ridiculous to me, and I often respond: "I won't if you don't."

There are several types of armed robbery — the most common three are listed below — but the chances of encountering any while you travel are slim. However, it's best to be forewarned and have a strategy in place in case you are ever a victim of violent crime.

Fight or flight

Your body is programmed with two possible responses for these emergency situations — fight or flight. There is a frozen moment as your body decides what to do, then you are geared to react: to try to bulldoze your way through the situation, or to try to get out of there as quickly as possible. However, during an armed robbery, the safest response is submission to the aggressor.

If you are a 'fight' type person, you really do need to control the urge to get smart, to resist and to fight back in situations like this. Let your belongings go, and do what you must to stay safe.

A highly trained military peacekeeper I knew was definitely programmed to fight. Confident in his instincts and his training, he argued with robbers who invaded his lodgings. Within minutes he was killed for protecting some cash. Hand the stuff over: the graveyards are full of dead heroes, but your bank balance can always be rebuilt.

Mugging

Mugging — street theft perpetrated by an armed criminal — is probably the most common violent crime one will encounter while travelling. The movie cliche of a sharp knife in a dark alley can be more real than we would like it to be.

The easiest way to avoid being mugged is to avoid the kind of places where muggings take place. Avoid quiet streets and dark alleys, especially late at night. Stay where there are crowds, passing traffic, and streetlights. Local knowledge can be invaluable; soon after you arrive at your destination, ask your concierge or at the tourist information desk if there are any areas that should be avoided during the day or at night. Mark these on your map for later reference, and stay away from them!

Of course not every quiet alley hides a mugger and not every crowd keeps you safe; likewise, it is impossible to always stay in well-lit areas with lots of people. If you become the victim of a mugger, stay calm and accede to their demands. It is better to lose your wallet than to be injured by a criminal's knife or gun.

Invasion

If violent criminals break into your home while you are there, you have become a victim of invasion. This type of crime can be particularly scary and traumatic because your personal space, your home, has been violated. It is just as bad if your hotel room or apartment is raided while you are travelling.

Some rooms are fitted with emergency alarms but if the opportunity arises to set off such an alarm, remember to put your safety first. You need to weigh up the security response time against the likelihood of being seen triggering the alarm. In general, your response to invaders should be the same as it would be to muggers: give them what they want and stay safe.

You probably won't want to stay in the same place after experiencing an invasion. This is a perfectly normal reaction. Your embassy may be able to assist you in choosing more-secure accommodation within your budget, or get you on to a flight home, if that is what you wish.

Hold-ups

Hold-ups can occur in any place which handles cash, alcohol or cigarettes. While some thieves will target stores who are open late at night, others will attempt hold-ups during the day at banks or similar institutions.

If you are somehow caught up in a hold-up, don't play the hero. Try to avoid contact with the criminals in order to avoid becoming a long-term hostage or too difficult to deal with. Criminals will deal with problem people in the quickest and easiest way they can; not thinking too much about future consequences. Trust me, you don't want to experience their "simple" solutions.

Surviving armed robbery

If you find yourself involved in an armed robbery, following some basic steps will reduce the risk of being injured. However, a positive result can't be guaranteed, even if you follow these suggestions to the letter. A lot depends on the criminal's state of mind and level of intoxication — you are at their whim.

- Remain calm and do not cry, beg or be over-emotional.

- Do not resist — you cannot outrun a bullet.

- Calmly hand over the items they want.

- Avoid eye contact. Eye contact can aggravate the criminal — it can be seen as a sign of aggression and also increases the chance of later recognition. They do not want to be caught — the punishment for such crimes in some countries is death.

- Make no sudden movements — they may think you are reaching for a weapon.

- Listen to the instructions and do what they want you to do — communication breakdowns can result in violence.

- The criminal is more nervous, more filled with adrenalin than you are — do not provoke them.

- Do not try to trick them, they may be smarter than you think.

In movies and TV shows, police detectives always ask if the victim can describe the thieves. While your description may be able to help police, there is no reason to take undue risks in getting it. The robber certainly doesn't want you to have a clear description of them, and security cameras can often do a better job than you. Just remember, the most important thing is to escape without injury.

Carjacking

Hijacking a vehicle, or carjacking, is a popular crime in much of Africa, although it also occurs throughout the world. The criminal's goal is to steal the car, and to achieve their goal they are often armed. The crime may or may not include kidnapping or harming the driver and other passengers.

The most simple deterrent to carjacking is to keep your doors locked. Depending on the level of threat, this might give you the few seconds you need to speed off and leave the criminal behind. As always, consider your safety first. You are unlikely to escape a gunshot at point-blank range, despite what happens in the movies.

An expert's tips

Carjacking was a common problem for humanitarian workers I was training in Africa, so the tips below are well tested! Many come from people who have experienced this frightening encounter first-hand.

I met a local driver during a training session who had survived being carjacked three times. While I'm never driving with him, his two quick-and-easy tips were:

- Always carry some small money in your top pocket so you can pass it over quickly. Sometimes a bribe was enough to stop the carjacking developing.

- Always carry cigarettes. He did not smoke, but they were always a great way to break the ice if the carjackers took him hostage.

I experienced an attempted car-jacking in a very remote area. I was with a local driver when we were ambushed at gun point, and since I didn't know the language the driver took over discussions with the aggressors. They were former soldiers, fully armed and very drunk. All they wanted was our car, but none of them could drive so they wanted a lift into the next town. Several days before, this group had ambushed another aid agency and the workers were still missing.

Our chances of surviving a lift into town were slim. After some heated discussion the group quickly backed off. I was befuddled — how had we got away? My quick-thinking driver had told them he was taking me to hospital: I had come down with a highly contagious disease, and he was scared about catching it himself! After a good look at my pasty colour they decided the car wasn't worth the risk, and let us pass. For once, my naturally pale complexion worked in my favour.

You can trust local people to cope very well if their life is also in danger, they are the experts in their country and know what is likely to placate a criminal.

The best procedure to follow is always the same: remain calm and give up your possessions. It's hard for some people to do, but these items can always be replaced. Are your possessions really worth losing your life over? Does your life have less value than your passport? Some money? A car?

Sexual assault

While the risk of sexual assault — for both men and women — is a real risk, it is important to remember that millions of people travel each year without being affected. You can certainly mitigate a lot of the risk by building the safety advice throughout this book into your daily habits, but — like any crime — there is no foolproof way to guarantee your safety.

Our advice: Before you go

- Go and travel… don't listen to the fear-mongers and naysayers.

- Research before you go. Look at the information bulletins published by your government, and for high-risk destinations consider obtaining a country-specific security briefing from a private company. Fearfree provide impartial, up-to-date bulletins like this, and they are not expensive.

- Register with your government's foreign affairs department or travel-tracking website, or contract a private security company to keep tabs on you.

- Plan your route so that you are not waiting in airports for any length of time. You should also plan the timing of your travel so that you are not transiting through or having to remain in airports during quiet periods, particularly at night.

- Plan ahead to avoid situations where you might become isolated in an unfamiliar environment.

- Try to find out as much as possible about the local culture, customs and expectations prior to your departure. Guidebooks, blogs and online forums are great resources.

Our advice: While you travel

- Try not to bring attention to yourself by offending local customs. Look at what others are doing, and mimic their look and behaviour to maintain the lowest profile possible.

- Be confident, or at least act confident.

- Trust your instinct to guide you away from dangerous scenarios. Act on those uncomfortable feelings or untoward advances by seeking help or removing yourself from the situation.

- Keep important contact numbers close at hand — both stored on your phone, and in a notebook or card in your wallet.

Arriving in a new country

You are at your most vulnerable upon arrival in a country, especially at night. Upon arrival at your destination, look for the person meeting you. If the person identified to meet you fails to turn up consider the following options:

- Call the hotel for information.

- Request assistance from an airport official or a police officer.

- Use a taxi if you know it is safe. Consider calling the hotel or a friend to let them know what's happening.

Two approaches to sexual assault

When running workshops the topic of sexual assault and female travel safety often arises. It must be in the back of every female traveller's mind, especially if you are a solo traveller. In several classes I have had the opportunity to hear stories of how female travellers have coped with attempted sexual assault. The following two stories relate real experiences, and demonstrate two very different reactions.

A European woman was in a remote city in North Africa. She was celebrating a local friend's promotion, enjoying some tea and cake with her friends at a mixed gathering of men and women at a guesthouse. The local police arrived, following a supposed report of illegal alcohol and prostitution. Kicking open the door of the house, they forced entry at gunpoint and started to beat the people inside the house. Two young officers dragged our woman outside by the hair. She was already protesting, but when they started to force her into a dark alleyway, she fought like hell: screaming, kicking and hitting out as she could. Although the two men tried to keep her quiet, the noise she made got the attention of a senior officer, who stopped the incident.

Not every potential victim is so lucky. In another workshop the subject of sexual assault was raised and another woman, a widow and former refugee, shared her experience. That night, as was customary, she slept with her children in a tent in the refugee camp. A group of men arrived, woke her and took her outside. She knew what they wanted, but she was more scared that her children would be harmed than she was about herself. She was submissive, she did not talk, scream or fight. She told us that her only thoughts were of survival for the sake of her children.

These women each reacted differently, but both showed amazing bravery in the face of an untenable situation.

Submit, or fight like hell

Even if you follow best practices for staying safe, the worst could still happen. There are two choices: submit, or fight like hell. It's a personal choice which needs to be made on the spot, depending on the location, the attackers and a dozen other variables. I have spoken to a number of victims who have used both strategies, and survived sexual assault.

If you are the victim of rape

If you are the victim of rape while travelling overseas, you should make contact with the authorities: for your medical safety if nothing else.

In countries with a predominantly western worldview, call the police. They are equipped and trained to help you, not only to deal with the perpetrators.

In some parts of Africa, Asia and the Middle East, your first point of contact should be your local embassy. We do not recommend you go straight to the police or another official source: you might receive terrible treatment from law enforcement officials. You may be incarcerated until the situation is resolved as rape victims are considered criminals in some places: having sex outside of marriage is considered the victim's fault regardless of the situation.

These laws are unfair to say the least, but your embassy should have the personnel, skills, and procedures to help you regardless of how you'd like to move forward.

Embassy staff are there to help you, not to force you through any legal or medical procedures you want to avoid. Many embassies carry emergency rape kits, or have access to well-trained doctors. In addition, they understand the legal system in the country, and can help you to press charges and find a lawyer if you wish.

If in doubt, contact your embassy first.

What impact does culture have on my safety?

For both women and men, it is very important to be aware of non-verbal actions which may invite unwanted attention. A friendly gesture or casual touch that is acceptable in your own culture may be viewed differently by other cultures and could put you at risk. In some cultures a woman making eye contact with a man is taken as a sign that she wants his attention.

Government officials in some locations may not be accustomed to women being in positions of authority or who act in a manner relative to their position. Your behaviour may be perceived as a masculine prerogative, and put you at risk from someone needing to assert their authority. It is unjust, but it is real, and you should research these risks and agree upon a strategy with your colleagues before arriving at your destination.

EMERGENCY RESPONSE

Dealing with disaster

Responding to an emergency

There is no perfect catch-all advice about how to respond to an emergency situation. Each event is unique, and your responses will be based on the best course of action you can find at the time. In this section, we outline general practices to help you reach the optimum decision.

While we will talk in more detail about reacting specifically to fire, floods and earthquakes, there are certain principles and ideas which you should always be aware of, which will help you in any emergency situation.

Create action plans

In some cases, waiting for rescue is not an option; staying still might put you at greater risk. It is important to be prepared to take some form of action and to think of escape or action plans as part of your everyday life. Professional sportspeople are always asking themselves how to attack or defend from their current position, even if the need isn't likely to arise; likewise, the safety-conscious traveller is always asking themselves how to get out of a situation as quickly and safely as possible.

In one of the cities I served in, major civil unrest was expected following an announcement about changes in the government. I prepared my apartment by bringing in extra food, water and provisions. I also arranged my "plan B" in case I needed to reach the UN compound quickly, or get to the airport for evacuation. I was aware that the UN emergency response team might be unable to help me, as more-important people and the wounded and sick would have higher priority than me, so I prepared a good supply of cash and an extra set of clothes in case I had to flee.

No emergency evacuation was needed that time, but I was ready with a plan, a backup plan, and the supplies I could reasonably expect to need.

While civil unrest isn't something you encounter every day, how would you deal with having to evacuate the building or city you are in?

Calling emergency services

Needless to say, you should find out the emergency services number of any country you visit. Program it into your mobile phone, but make sure you remember it too. When calling for help, remember "the five W's". Talking about each of these will help to pass on the most important information to emergency services.

- **Who** are you?

- **What** are you calling about?

- **Where** are you?

- **When** did the incident happen?

- **Why** do you need help?

Train yourself to:

- Know the local emergency number.

- Know the location of exits in any vehicle or building you are in.

- Sketch out mental plans for potential emergencies.

- Seat yourself in a place you can move from quickly.

Nobody can predict when a disaster might happen, or how serious the effects will be, but we can all be a little more prepared — even when on the road. Every time you pack your bags, run through the checklist above to refresh your memory: these habits will help to ensure your safety in a disaster.

Fire

Fires are all-the-more dangerous if you are high up in a modern hotel, office or apartment building. Although smoke-stop doors and other fire-prevention methods are designed into our buildings, the higher you are, the further you have to travel before you get out.

When staying in a large hotel, request a room between the second and fourth floor of the building, which will allow for a quick exit in the case of an emergency. Choosing a room close to the stairwell will mean you are that much closer to the way out.

In case of fire

While every fire plan is different, these three steps should always come first:

- Activate an alarm to warn others and to trigger automatic emergency responses.
- Evacuate the building.
- Give detailed information about the fire to staff members and emergency services.

Getting away

As you evacuate:

- Walk, do not run.
- Obey the instructions of staff and emergency service personnel.

- Always use the stairs. Elevators tend to malfunction during fires and may open onto floors where the fire has caught hold or has already caused structural damage.
- Stay in single file in stairways. Emergency staff may need to come up as you descend.
- Stay as calm as you can. Don't panic, and try to keep others calm around you as well.

A crush or human stampede can be just as dangerous as the fire you are trying to escape. Try to move quickly but calmly, urging others to do the same, removing obstacles as you go.

Too smoky?

Amazingly, smoke can travel up to 300 feet per minute. Air will be clearer lower down, so keep your head low or crawl along the floor when moving through smoky areas.

If smoke is coming from under a door, there might be greater danger on the other side. If you are unsure about any pathway:

- Feel the closed door with the back of your hand.
- Do not open hot doors: the extra oxygen will fuel an already-raging fire.
- Find another way to exit the building.

When trapped by fire

It is always better to find a way to evacuate a burning building than to stay where you are and wait to be rescued. However, if you find yourself trapped in a room, give yourself the best chance of survival.

- Block all gaps around the doors using wet towels. This prevents smoke from entering the room.

- Do not break open a window unless you have no other choice. An open window can allow smoke to enter the room.

- Run a bath full of water and allow it to overflow.

- Keep dowsing hot spots and the towels around your door with cold water.

- If flames enter the room and there's no way to escape, protect the bathroom as long as you can.

- Submerge yourself in the bath to protect yourself from fire.

Flooding

Flash floods, caused by storms or failed engineering, are unpredictable and almost impossible to react to once they have started. A lot of the time, however, we can see flood conditions developing before they happen.

If you think an area might flood — if there are high seas, strong rain or local warnings — change your plans and stay away. If you are in the area, take the opportunity to move on. There's no point going somewhere that's preparing for a natural disaster unless you really have to.

Dealing with a flood

- Seek shelter indoors or high ground, if in the open.

- Turn off electrical and gas supplies at the mains to reduce the chance of electrocution or poisoning.

- Don't drink anything from the tap.

- Don't use wet/soaked appliances.

- Move all your things up as high as possible in your shelter.

- Don't play in or move unnecessarily through flood water: who knows what's in it, or what is invisible under the water.

- Follow the directions of the locals and local emergency services.

- Look after yourself, your family, your travel companions, then anyone else… in that order.

A note on monsoon season

From June to October South East Asia experiences the monsoon season — torrential rain falls for days and an unbelievable volume of water starts to pile up. With tropical storms hitting dry earth, whatever drainage exists is quickly overpowered: flash flooding damages towns, roads are washed out, and rivers rise quickly and dangerously. If you choose to travel in South East Asia during monsoon season, expect delays and problems caused by heavy rains.

The additional stagnant water and tropical heat is a breeding ground for mosquitos and other bugs, which may carry diseases. Disease risk is high during and immediately after the monsoon rains.

Earthquakes and explosions

In the last two years, I've been lucky enough to avoid two major earthquakes by several hundred kilometres: one centred in Concepción, Chile, the other in Christchurch, New Zealand. Both cost hundreds of lives, and the close calls certainly made me think about how I would have reacted had I been closer to the scene of the disaster.

Although earthquakes and explosions are very different events, the aftermath is similar and your response to the situation should follow the same lines. In both cases:

- Stay calm.

- Take shelter under a hard surface such as a desk or table. Use a doorframe if nothing else is available.

- Stay away from windows, which might implode.

- Exit buildings as soon as you can.

- Move to clear ground, away from buildings and trees.

- Stay low, even lying on the ground during aftershocks.

Every big earthquake has its own horror stories, and some of them are recurring patterns that waste lives needlessly. After running into the street to avoid the danger of one tremor, a Christchurch resident went back into her shop to collect her cellphone. An aftershock caused the building to come down around her.

Strong aftershocks can occur for days after a big quake, and can destroy or further damage buildings — even those that showed no outward signs of damage from the initial quake. Do not re-enter buildings until local authorities have deemed it safe to do so, no matter how valuable the belongings left inside.

If trapped in debris

In October 2011, a 7.2 magnitude earthquake hit eastern Turkey, with the city Ercis particularly hard-hit. Hundreds died, but even three days later people were still being found and rescued from within the rubble of buildings — there is always hope. If trapped:

- Avoid movement so that you do not kick up dust.

- Cover your nose and mouth with anything you can find to hand to filter dust.

- Tap on a pipe or wall so rescue services can hear and locate you.

- Shout only as a last resort, as shouting can cause you to inhale dangerous particles in the air and drain your energy.

- If you have any type of electronic communication device, make sure to conserve battery life. If you have made contact with potential rescuers, arrange to turn it on at certain times to communicate with them. If battery life and the communications networks allow, change your voicemail so people know that you are alive, and where you are trapped.

Those trapped and needing rescue might have a long wait ahead of them. Try to stay calm, keep your morale high, and encourage anyone else trapped with you to do the same.

After a disaster

The hours and days following a disaster can be more dangerous than the initial event. We recommend that travellers leave the area as soon as it becomes feasible.

The initial response efforts are targeted at rescuing people who are trapped, and making the area safe. Unless you have specialist skills, you are just another person to look after, rather than being helpful. Volunteer labour will certainly be needed during the cleanup and rebuilding phases, but that may not start for a week or more.

Communication

Natural disasters often damage electricity and communication lines, and the flood of calls and messages will overload any remaining infrastructure. This means you may not be able to call or get online reliably or at all. When possible, contact one or two key people, and ask them to pass on your news and situation to others — including to your nation's embassy or consulate, who will be trying to locate their citizens. If you have access to voicemail, record a message saying you are OK. This will be a great relief to callers if your phone runs out of battery or cannot connect to the network.

Use social networks like Facebook to announce your situation, and ask people to monitor your wall and respond to those asking after your wellbeing. In addition to taking much of the pressure off you, you'll be reducing the stress for many of your family members, friends and colleagues.

Food, water and other necessities

Communication lines are not the only thing that go down: important transport lines get cut too, and that means food, water, fuel and other supplies start to dry up very quickly.

When the Concepción earthquake hit Chile in 2010, we were in the resort town of Puerto Varas, about 600 kilometres south of the epicentre. We woke to around 90 seconds of heavy shaking, which seemed to last for several minutes. We checked that our travel group was safe, and went back to sleep.

When we woke up in the morning, we were glad to find that water and gas were still running, and the water was clear and smelled fine. We could make hot drinks on the stove, and after a coffee two of our party headed down into the township. We wanted to see how people were reacting — if they seemed stressed about food supplies or anything else that might spell trouble. Luckily people were calm: shopping for non-perishable food and queuing for petrol, but there were no signs of the looting we later saw on TV. We bought a few days' worth of food, tried to get as much information as possible, and planned out our next couple of days.

After any natural disaster, it's important to look after yourself, your group, then the people around you. Stay alert to changing attitudes and potential dangers — whether that is contaminated water or people becoming panicked and potentially violent. Do what you can to stay safe, and remove yourself from the danger area.

ACCIDENTAL WARZONES

From riots to terrorist attacks

Demonstrations and riots

While travelling from Istanbul to Kirsehir in central Turkey, we took the opportunity to stop for half a day in the capital, Ankara. There weren't really any tourist hotspots we wanted to check out: we just wanted to see what the central city looked like and to take the opportunity to visit the mausoleum of Kemal Ataturk. He was a shrewd commander who turned back the ANZAC forces at Gallipoli, then dragged Ottoman Turkey into the modern world following World War One. Who wouldn't want to see that?

We emerged from a train station around a kilometre from the mausoleum. A large group, adorned with red scarves and patches and carrying red flags, was gathering around the station, many shouting angrily. We decided we wanted none of that, and started walking away in what we hoped was the right direction, stopping after we had walked a little distance to check our map. As we continued towards the mausoleum, we saw TV crews setting up to catch the action. This seemed like an ominous sign.

"What's going on?" I asked a news cameraman. "Is this going to get dangerous?" Assured that the political protest wouldn't get violent, we did visit Ataturk's mausoleum, along with an estimated 15,000 of our closest Turkish friends. It probably wasn't the smartest idea ever, but it worked out in the end.

When protests turn into riots

The problem with protests, as non-violent as they might start off, is that they are unpredictable. There's something strange about the human psyche which makes us react differently when we're in a large crowd. Emotions get amplified and a bad decision can turn a peaceful gathering into a stampede or into a massive brawl. It is our advice that, when you are unsure of how things stand or if you are unable to understand instructions and warnings, you should stay away.

If anti-riot police or armed forces are deployed by the government to control or suppress a demonstration, it is imperative that you not get caught up in the crowds. Leave the heroic camerawork to the professionals: media organisations tend to look after their own in these situations, but who is looking after you? Local law enforcement and the protestors themselves won't be.

If rioting begins:

- Take shelter at your hotel or office.

- If you are unable to reach a known safe place, try taking shelter in a store or private house.

- Do not go out to get the 'feel' of the situation.

- Consider evacuating the area sooner rather than later.

- Avoid becoming part of the crowd in the demonstration. Military or riot police won't differentiate between you and a rioter.

Definitions

Unexploded Ordnance (UXO) are explosive items that have been left behind, improperly disposed of, or launched but failed to explode. Like the hand grenade of the story, rockets, grenades, mortars and cluster munitions are often found by children or farmers with deadly and debilitating results.

Landmines are often called 'the perfect soldier'. They sit in the ground for years, never needing food, water or shelter. The older they get, the more sensitive they become to movement — hence more dangerous. There are over 600 different types of landmines, not including the crudely improvised versions. In general, they are separated into two groups: anti-people and anti-vehicle.

Anti-people mines are generally small and designed to maim and severely injure. They are usually activated by weight, vibration, tripwire or by manual control.

Anti-vehicle mines are generally activated by extreme pressure from weights of 120kg or more. As time passes they can become more sensitive as a result of age, environmental conditions and location. This means smaller weights can also lead to an explosion: dancing or posing on them is not recommended despite the theoretical safety.

Things that go boom

You never imagined that explosives might play a part in your travels, but there is an inestimable amount of unexploded ordnance left in fields, in forests and even in cities around the world.

I was once in a remote outdoor market buying fresh produce when a young child wanted my attention. He was showing me his new and probably only toy — an unexploded hand grenade. Not exactly what most kids would ask for for Christmas.

As I had next to no command of the language, I used body language to try and communicate the risk without startling him. I managed to wave over a local police officer who took the situation in hand. Luckily this story doesn't end with a bang, but what if the child had panicked? What if he had thrown it, or pulled the release pin — just for fun?

Understanding dangerous areas

It is obviously better to avoid these deadly items! In most areas official warning signs exist, normally written in the local language, but with the international symbol of a red sign with a white skull and crossbones. Guidebooks and online travel guides will often mention the risk of UXO in an area.

Local residents will often know where dangers exist and they will have a "know sign" such as two crossed sticks, a pile of rocks, or a warning flag. Without a local guide, it is best to trust your gut feeling: the warning might be current or out of date, it might be for mines, snakes or some other threat. Always be cautious and respect local knowledge.

If there has been military activity or large-scale fighting, there may be abandoned military bunkers, vehicles or equipment. Avoid these areas, no matter how tempting the souvenir or photo opportunity may be. The area may be intentionally booby-trapped or contain UXO.

A young soldier in the Balkans found this out the hard way when he climbed into an abandoned MIG Jetfighter lying derelict on the side of a runway. He climbed into the cockpit, waved for the camera, and sat down. The ejector seat was still primed and, somehow, it activated — sending the poor soldier up into the air and leaving him with a broken back.

Do not try this at home

The following myths, made popular by movies and TV, need to be re-examined.

- If you stand on a mine and hear a click, slowly removing your weight will not keep you safe. There is no second click, there is only a boom.

- You cannot retrace your steps out of a minefield. It is impossible to completely and accurately walk backwards following your footsteps.

- You cannot outrun an explosive blast, even if you are a sprinter. It is impossible to move faster than an explosive's shockwave.

- A area cannot be cleared by letting livestock roam around. It takes days for professional mine action staff to clear an area inch by inch.

You should know:

- First and foremost, avoid potential danger areas. Combat tourism is best left for soldiers.

- If you encounter an item that looks military, it probably is. Do not touch it, and definitely do not play with it like a football.

- Never take explosives as a souvenir.

- Avoid having a look inside a bunker, tank or combat aircraft. They may be rigged with traps.

- Be aware that explosives don't always look like you would expect. Many children are hurt each year by explosives hidden inside an attractive cover, such as a teddy bear or toy.

Stuck in a minefield

If you are unlucky enough to find yourself in a minefield, stop and wait for assistance. It is better to wait for help for a few hours than risk a lifetime without limbs.

If someone with you is trapped or injured, stay calm. Do not act the hero and rush over: there may well be more landmines or UXO nearby. Reassure your companion and get help by calling or leaving the scene to find assistance.

Unnecessary lives are taken each year by people trying to assist others in a minefield, and they themselves become a victim. Instead of rushing over to assist the victim, provide them with verbal instructions to stay where they are, and not to move. Communication from any distance may be difficult as a blast can damage both hearing and vision.

Minefields and unexploded weapons are extremely dangerous – caution cannot be highlighted enough.

All of this advice came to mind as I travelled through Cambodia — a land severely damaged by Pol Pot and the recent wars throughout South East Asia. We had hired a guide to help us explore the countryside around Battambang — a provincial capital in the north-west of the country. We visited several temples that day, and in the surrounding jungle — on each side of the path — were several signs warning of landmines. Thinking they might be exaggerating the risk, I asked the guide how close landmines might be to the pathway. They might be within five or ten meters, he said: although the paths and nearby surroundings had been swept, there were not enough resources to fully de-mine the area.

Several organisations, such as UNICEF, work to remove landmines from all over the world, with the aim of clearing the Earth completely. According to some sources, over 100,000 landmines are removed from the ground worldwide each year. However, at this rate, it will take 1100 more years to completely rid the earth of landmines. You will encounter the risk of UXO whenever you travel in a country that has seen war: keep your eye out for the warning signs and stay away from potential dangers.

Terrorism and your travels

One of the questions we get asked most often by short-term and first-time travellers is about the dangers of terrorist action when away from home. This makes sense because the media seems fascinated by terrorism and reports on it whenever possible, increasing the perceived risk and making regular travellers scared of leaving their home country. However, perceived risk is often just this: perceived. Travellers almost always think the risk of terrorist attack is much greater than it actually is.

Terrorists are people with an overwhelming urge to be destructive and cause grief and misery to ordinary citizens. Often their cause is difficult for most people to understand, and in some cases is disrespectful to the very people they claim to be fighting for. In some people's eyes they are freedom fighters championing a cause: it all depends what side of the fence you are on.

But how does the recent increase of terrorism affect your travel? Hopefully not much! Longer queues and more difficult security screenings at airports is the only sign most of us ever see when it comes to the terrorist threat.

Terrorism isn't new, and isn't likely

Terrorism is not new. Even in our home country of New Zealand we celebrate Guy Fawkes Night, which is in effect the commemoration of a failed terrorist plot. Guy Fawkes was a man who plotted to — and almost succeeded in — blowing up the English Parliament way back in 1605. He was a freedom fighter to some; a criminal to others.

Sadly, terrorism hasn't gone away since then, but travel (and most of life) is now is much safer than it was back in the seventeenth century, and a heck of a lot easier too!

To be concerned about the risks of travel is understandable, but it is seldom less safe than stepping out of your front door. If you live in a large urban city, you're likely to be travelling somewhere with a lower crime rate than normal and, assuming you are not travelling through hostile regions, there's also less chance of you encountering terror attacks.

What does a terror criminal look like?

I wish I knew! Every law enforcement and intelligence officer wishes they knew the answer, and I bet you do too. The simple fact is that terrorists come in all shapes, sizes, colours, religions and ages. There's no way to profile a terrorist based on any standard criterion.

Being shot at

When bullets start to fly, it's hard to keep your composure. It is a shocking experience that slows your reactions and can leave you stunned. If you are caught up in a situation where weapon fire is being exchanged, get to a safer place and do all you can to stay calm.

- Get low and hide.

- Don't cross open ground.

- Stay calm and think clearly.

- Wait it out: don't treat a lull like a ceasefire.

If you are in the open, get down and take shelter in a ditch, drain or hollow impression in the ground. Solid cover, such as a brick wall, is always better.

If you are in a vehicle, you have two choices: either get as low as you can, or exit the vehicle. Getting down low, on the floor, minimises your chances of being hit. Exiting the vehicle might allow you to find better safety or try to evade the shooters; when exiting the vehicle, always leave from the side facing away from those firing. Formulate a quick plan to get to the nearest available cover before moving.

Most people will react automatically: hitting the ground and moving towards shelter, and away from the source of fire. Don't fight this reaction — go with it. Stopping to think about what to do next might leave you shocked into not moving at all.

Surviving an explosion

Rocket fire is seldom as prolific as gunfire, but does vast amounts of damage. I was in an embassy in the Middle East some years ago when all of a sudden rockets went past the window of our second-level office. My colleague and I raced down to the basement and pulled our protective gear on without a word or second thought. Adrenaline and our reactions dictated our actions, and they will dictate yours as well.

What to do

- Head away from probable targets.

- Seek shelter and remain there until help arrives.

- If caught in the open, immediately lie flat and cover your head.

- If inside, seek shelter in the basement.

Another colleague, a senior British police officer, was caught outside in the open when a rocket landed close to him. He hit the deck very quickly and avoided the majority of the blast, but the oxygen was sucked out of his lungs by the implosion. After the attack he rose, casually dusted himself off and made a cup of tea! Maybe there's something to be said for stereotypes. His advice: always close your mouth — the amount of dirt in the air will be intense.

Luck plays a large part in surviving any exchange of weapon fire, and the bigger the rounds the less chance you will escape unscathed. The best recommendation we can give is to avoid potential trouble spots, but if caught up in such a situation stay calm and stay low.

Chemical attack

Chemical weapons may be used by terrorists or military groups in order to efficiently but indiscriminately kill a large number of people, destroy food or water sources, or to remove access to hiding places.

Chemicals may be introduced to a water or food supply, or released into the air. While it's extremely unlikely that you will ever face any kind of chemical attack, if you do:

- Evacuate to higher ground or upwind.

- If inside, seal the room and cover yourself with a blanket.

- Use an air mask if you have access to one, or filter your breathing through a shirt or other fabric.

- Seek medical treatment immediately.

- If you have access to clean water, wash clean any exposed skin.

In this section, we've discussed everything from protests turning violent to terrorist attacks, and everything in between. The chance of a traveller — especially a tourist — ever getting caught up in these events is very low. Remember, travel is generally safe and tens of thousands of people travel each year without incident.

It's our job, however, to ensure you are prepared if you do find yourself — accidentally — in a war zone. It's best to revise this section before any trip to keep the correct reactions clear in your mind, and employ safety professionals if you have reason to believe you are heading into a dangerous situation.

YOUR GOOD HEALTH

Basic first aid for travellers

It must be stressed we are not medical professionals, and we accept no liability for your health! These are the things we have discovered as we travel around the world and we hope they are useful to you.

An important part of your pre-trip preparation is investigating current medical risks prevalent in your destinations. Your first port of call is the **World Health Organisation (WHO) website**[4], and you should also consult a specialist travel doctor, or a GP if one isn't available.

The WHO website has all sorts of useful medical information, including updates about new diseases and current outbreaks. Every year, all around the world, new sicknesses are being discovered — usually by poor unsuspecting citizens, rather than by scientists! For example, an unknown disease is causing quiet havoc in Rajasthan, India at the time of writing. The WHO website will warn you about such problems, but the chances of you getting caught up in an outbreak while travelling are slim. The most common medical issues faced by travellers are the same problems they face at home: cuts and scratches and different strains of everyday diseases.

Vaccinations

Regardless of where you are travelling or what heath risks exist (or don't appear to exist), you must make time to visit a doctor with a copy of your itinerary before you go. We recommend you do this at least three months before you leave, as some vaccinations require a series of several shots in order to be effective.

While corporate travellers should have their health preparations covered by the company, individuals and family travellers will probably have to pay through the nose for the consultations and vaccinations needed. Check with your health insurance company to see if they will cover this pre-emptive treatment. It is also worth noting many clinics charge a reduced rate for groups, so a couple or family consultation will cost less than each individual going alone.

Your doctor can advise you about which vaccinations you should have, based on your itinerary. If you're planning more trips in the

---

[4] http://www.who.int/en/

near future, it might be worth considering receiving vaccinations for these destinations at the same time, in order to save time and to avoid having to pay another consultation fee. Use your time with the travel doctor wisely: ask about any other travel health questions you have. At minimum, bring up malaria, rabies and any personal concerns.

Some countries' entry and visa requirements mean you must have a Yellow Fever certificate if you have recently visited certain high-risk countries (mostly in South America and Africa). If you get the vaccination, make sure you get the certificate and take it with you when you travel.

Regular medicines

Ensure that you have a prescription for any regular medication you need. Having a prescription will not only help you find it in your destination countries, but will also smooth your way through customs, proving to officials that you will use the drugs you are carrying.

That said, illegal drugs are illegal whether you have a prescription or not. It doesn't matter if your doctor says you can take marijuana for medical reasons, carrying even a small quantity is illegal in most of the world. Similarly, codeine is sold over the counter in many countries, but it's illegal in Greece: leave it at home. Ask your doctor about the international legality of your medications and if you can buy more overseas. If your doctor isn't 100% sure, do the research yourself online.

Drugs are sold under different names in different countries. It's not a different medicine, it's just a licensing and branding issue. Find out the generic names of the medicines you're likely to want, as well as some local brand names if possible, so that you can identify them when you need to.

If you have a medical need to carry syringes on a plane with you, make sure your doctor gives you a letter stating this. It is nearly impossible to take syringes on any mainstream flight without one.

Eye care

Make sure you leave home with a relatively up-to-date prescription in case you need replacement glasses or contact lenses. Some people carry a cheap replacement pair of glasses with them, but we tend to just rely on contact lenses if anything was to go wrong. Contact lenses are easily available almost everywhere you find a major city — or buy online if you have a week or longer at one address.

Not every prescription is available everywhere, even if it seems remarkably normal. I use daily disposable contact lenses produced by major international brand, and, although the brand is very popular in Argentina, I can't find their daily disposable lenses for love or money.

It's common sense, but if you have an unusual prescription or you're heading into the wilderness for an extended period, do your research on how to source replacement glasses and contacts before leaving.

After arrival

Once you have arrived at your destination some simple health precautions will help to ensure your future safety: be aware of health services, eat and drink safe foods, and treat symptoms early.

Do you know the local emergency number? Is it saved on your mobile phone? Having access to the local emergency number may save your life, and it only takes a minute to find out. If you are staying in one place for a while, locate a local medical centre or hospital. This is especially worth doing if you're travelling in an isolated or less-developed area.

Eat safe foods

Foods like fruit should be washed and well-dried before eating. Meals should be freshly prepared and served on clean, dry dishes. If you can, ascertain whether the food has been stored correctly before serving and whether it has been freshly prepared or reheated. Even fresh food can become dangerous if prepared in unhygienic conditions, and eating it can lead to serious problems.

Water is also an important issue. If you know that water is not safe to drink, ensure that all plates and cutlery are completely dry before eating off them. It is also best to avoid ice, unless you know that it has been professionally prepared from clean water. Various lightweight water filters are available to reduce the need to constantly buy bottled water.

Traveller's diarrhoea, whether it is called Delhi belly or Montezuma's revenge, is a common complaint. Sometimes this is just the body's way of coping with rigorous travel and the new diet, but sometimes it can develop into acute food poisoning. There is no doubt that this can be dangerous: in 2011 a young New Zealand backpacker died from food poisoning contracted in Thailand. This case brings into focus two important general health and safety concepts: be careful of what you eat and treat symptoms as soon as possible.

Treat symptoms early

While travelling, it's important to be aware of your body and deal with sicknesses early, before they have the chance to develop into something more serious. Most of the time a cold is just a cold, but small symptoms could be a sign of a more-serious disease. If anything, you should err on the side of caution since the 'simple solution' you'd use at home may not be available. The issue might also be more acute than you expect — traveller's D might develop into serious food poisoning, tiredness could be a sign of meningitis, or an infected cut could quickly escalate into blood poisoning.

On the label of almost every medicine bottle is the instruction "if symptoms persist, seek medical advice". This is certainly the case when you are travelling. Listen to your body, act appropriately, and don't be afraid to spend your insurance company's money on medical advice.

Your first-aid kit

Carrying a basic first-aid kit will allow you to quickly react to minor issues and will save you the inconvenience of trawling your hotel for a sticking plaster after a minor scratch.

At the least, we recommend packing the following in a waterproof, crush-resistant container:

- General items: tweezers, scissors or a multi-tool, a small torch, safety pins, sunscreen, matches, thermometer, insect repellent, a sewing kit, painkillers

- For diarrhoea: imodium tablets and hydration mixes

- Bleeding: crepe and pressure bandages

- Blisters: assorted plasters/band aids

- Breaks: triangular bandage

- Infections: antibiotics, disinfectant, antiseptic cream, isopropyl alcohol wipes

- Allergies: antihistamines and an EpiPen if prescribed

Consider carrying a small first-aid book. If you have a Kindle or smartphone, several travel-related health books are available for download.

If you are travelling with carry-on luggage only, you will have to leave the scissors or multi-tool behind. Consider buying a replacement once you arrive at your destination.

FURTHER RESOURCES

Travel Safety was co-written by Craig Bidois and Craig Martin. Together they maintain a Facebook group with daily updates on travel and security issues. You can get free access at **http://facebook.com/travelsafety**.

In addition, visit the authors' websites at:

http://travelsafetybook.com

http://fearfree.co.nz

http://indietravelpodcast.com/travelsafety

Each website has further resources and links to help you travel well.

If you'd like to give us feedback about this book or if there something you'd like included in the next edition, visit:

http://travelsafetybook.com/feedback

If you have encountered a scam, set-up or other dastardly plot, you can share it with other travellers at **http://indietravelpodcast.com/travelsafety** where you can also get free membership in the Indie Travel Podcast Community.

Remember to join us at **http://facebook.com/travelsafety**. We look forward to hearing from you.

fearfree
security and safety
management

If you are in business, your health and safety obligations extend to staff travelling abroad.

Minimise risk for your valuable staff members and minimise the risk of non-compliance with our affordable packages of training solutions, travel security updates, and destination-specific travel reports.

We're here to help!

The world of security can be grim at times, but it doesn't have to be scary. Contact Fearfree today, and our friendly staff can put together a professional action plan to help you and your business stay safe.

+64 226 246 311
or 0800 332 737 in New Zealand

info@fearfree.co.nz

http://fearfree.co.nz

Other books from
INDIE TRAVEL MEDIA

The Art of Solo Travel:
A girls' guide to long-term travel

by Stephanie Lee

"It is time to stop dreaming your life and start living your dreams": this is the philosophy behind Stephanie Lee's new book "The Art of Solo Travel – A Girls' Guide". This is not just a guide for solo female travelers, but an invaluable source of practical tips on how to manage a small budget on the road and on how to appreciate your time abroad by yourself.

Angela Corrias, Travel Calling

While they tend to be sincere in their enthusiasm and generous in their advice, sometimes it can be hard for seasoned travel veterans to express what it's like to leave behind the structure of a "normal" life and embark on a game-changing adventure. Art of Solo Travel: A Girls' Guide by Stephanie Lee answers that question. In fact, I found it hard to think of a question she DIDN'T answer. Stephanie has a unique ability to go back in time to the point at which she not only made the decision to travel extensively, but also how she prepared for it – and then explain it all to you, step by step.

Christine Cantera, Galavanting

http://artofsolotravel.com

Download a free sample
from **Amazon.com** or **Amazon.co.uk**

Art of Couples' Travel:
Your guide to long-term travel together

by Craig and Linda Martin
with Jessica Ainley and Daniela Heinrich

Art of Couples' Travel is extremely useful. I wish I had something similar when we began planning for our trip! The gadgets and insurance section were especially helpful to us since we still need to figure out those things before we leave on our travels.

Kim, So Many Places

What I love about The Art of Couples Travel is that there is no sugar coating. Craig and Linda tell it like it is and provide you with useful, honest and practical ways to travel as a couple. Their honesty is refreshing as they show other couples that long term travel is a realistic (and amazing) lifestyle. Their love of travel is infectious and they are eager to share it with everyone."

Ant and Elise, Positive World Travel

Traveling happily as a couple is an art form. Craig and Linda have put together a great primer for couples thinking about making travel dreams a reality. It's loaded with great no-nonsense advice from a couple that's been there and survived to tell the story!

Danny and Jillian, I Should Log Off

http://artofcouplestravel.com

Download a free sample
from **Amazon.com** or **Amazon.co.uk**

How to Live Like Us: Travel around the world

by Craig and Linda Martin

As full-time round-the-world travellers, we are often asked one question: How do you do it?

"How to live like us" is an attempt to answer how we can travel around the world. We deal with saving to leave, the cost of full-time travel against living at 'home', and practical details about living on the road as a couple.

Since 2006, Craig and Linda Martin have visited over 50 countries and have made what many believe to be an impossible dream -- fully funded, location independent travel. They run the Indie Travel Podcast.

http://indietravelpodcast.com/books

Download a free sample
from **Amazon.com** or **Amazon.co.uk**

TRAVELLING EUROPE

by Craig Martin

Everything from "Can I afford it?" to "How to save for it?" to "What should we do if we take the kids?", 'Travelling Europe' made me want to get back on the road. There's a lot of high-quality information packed into this little book, and many little gems of information that only come from an author who *lives* travelling. The book is as the podcast: smart, not smarmy.

KC Greene

There's a number of travel bloggers who are location-independent. Not all of us can make that leap, and some want to live vicariously through them. But where would you start planning if you wanted to? Fortunately, Craig and Linda Martin break it down for you fairly granularly, from the rule of thirds when it comes to travel budgets, making money while abroad and getting around in order to keep up this lifestyle...

The book is a little more than a 4 star book and is a few ticks short of a 5 star book, however. It's worth buying and lending to friends and might make a good gift for recent college grads.

N. Hawkins "Where is Hawkins"

http://indietravelpodcast.com/books

Download a free sample
from **Amazon.com** or **Amazon.co.uk**

Coming up

Travel Safety online training program

Las Vegas city guide

Buenos Aires city guide

Auckland city guide

Solo travel for the baby boomer

Career break handbook

How to live like a local

Stay up to date at
http://indietravelpodcast.com/books

CPSIA information can be obtained at www.ICGtesting.com
Printed in the USA
BVOW010319130313

315300BV00029B/703/P